A2 Business Studies

UNIT 5w

AQA

Business Report and Essay

John Wolinski

Philip Allan Updates
Market Place
Deddington
Oxfordshire
OX15 0SE

tel: 01869 338652
fax: 01869 337590
e-mail: sales@philipallan.co.uk
www.philipallan.co.uk

© Philip Allan Updates 2001

ISBN 0 86003 496 8

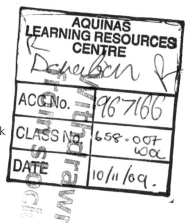

This Guide has been written specifically to support students preparing for the AQA Business Studies Unit 5W examination. The content has been neither approved nor endorsed by AQA and remains the sole responsibility of the author.

Typeset by Good Imprint, West Sussex
Printed by Information Press, Eynsham, Oxford

Contents

Introduction

■ ■ ■

Business reports

■ ■ ■

Essay questions

Introduction

About this guide

This Student Unit Guide has been written with one objective in mind: to provide you with the ideal resource for your revision of AQA Unit 5W, A2 Business Studies. After this introductory note on the aims and assessment of A-level, the guide is divided into two sections to provide questions and answers to both the business report and the essay aspects of Unit 5W.

Unlike other guides in the series, this book does not provide reference on the subject content. This is because Unit 5W tests the whole range of the A2 specification. Although the AQA specification identifies topics as AS or A2, a close scrutiny of the details will reveal that many AS topics can be extended in the A2 modules. Furthermore, the introduction to A2 Module 6 states that it 'builds on all the AS subject content . . .' Thus, although there will be a predominance of A2 subject content tested in Unit 5W, the specification allows questions to be set on any part of the specification from both the AS and the A2 modules. Students are advised to revise all of the AS and A2 specification in preparation for Unit 5W.

The first section of this guide provides six questions in the form of business reports. Question 1 is based solely on coverage of the AS modules, but subsequent questions are based mainly on A2 content. Each question is based on the format of the A2 papers and is followed by one or two sample answers (an A-grade and a lower-grade response) interspersed with examiner's comments.

The second section provides six questions in the form of essays. Each question is based on the format of the A2 papers and is followed by one or two sample answers (an A-grade and a lower-grade response) interspersed with examiner's comments.

You should check that you are aware of the subject content before attempting the question from the question and answer sections, and only read the specimen answers after you have tackled the question yourself.

Aims of the A-level qualification

A-level Business Studies aims to encourage candidates to:
- develop a critical understanding of organisations, the markets they serve and the process of adding value
- be aware that business behaviour can be studied from the perspectives of a range of stakeholders including customers, managers, creditors, owners/shareholders and employees
- acquire a range of skills, including decision-making and problem-solving
- be aware of current business structure and practice

Assessment

AS and A2 papers are designed to test certain skills. **Every mark that is awarded on**

an AS or A2 paper is given for the demonstration of a skill. The content of the course (the theories, concepts and ideas) is there to provide a framework to allow you to show your skills — recognising the content on its own is not enough to merit high marks.

The following skills are tested:
- **Knowledge and understanding** — recognising and describing business concepts and ideas.
- **Application** — being able to explain or apply your understanding.
- **Analysis** — developing a line of thought in order to demonstrate its impact or consequences.
- **Evaluation** — making a judgement by weighing up the evidence provided.
- **Synthesis** — building the parts of an argument into a connected whole, developing a logical sequence of argument, and demonstrating clarity through summarising.

Unit 5W: Business Report and Essay has a much higher weighting for the higher-level skill of evaluation than any paper other than Unit 6 (the case study). Bear this in mind during your preparation and revision, as you will need to practise developing arguments more fully for this paper. This will be good practice for the case study too, which has a similar, higher weighting for these skills. The units have been designed to allow you to develop your skills as you progress through the course.

It should be recognised that this unit is an alternative to the coursework option, and is thus assessed in a similar way. The business report is designed to test your ability to synthesise data (recognise the value of specific pieces of information) and then to analyse and evaluate that information. The essay provides you with a choice of one from four titles, and will enable you to discuss a broad business issue in some depth.

Your preparation for this unit should be different from AS. The ability to demonstrate (a) knowledge and (b) application is less important (20% weighting rather than 30% in AS). Similarly, the weighting for analysis is reduced from 24% to 20%.

The major change is in Assessment Objective 4 (evaluation and synthesis) which is increased from 16% (AS) to 40% (this unit). Note that although there is 40% weighting for Assessment Objective 4 in both Units 5 and Unit 6 (the case study), the break-down of this skill is very different. In Unit 6, all 40% is for evaluation (judgement); in Unit 5, 12.5% is for synthesis, with 27.5% for evaluation.

In Unit 5 there will only be two questions. Both of these will require considerable evaluation (judgement). In the business report this should be in the form of a reasoned recommendation, but in the essay an overall judgement on the topic chosen is required.

Practise the specimen questions in this book as part of your revision. This will help you to discover the different needs of the paper.

The examination paper for Unit 5 has a fixed mark scheme. The marks for each skill in each question are awarded as follows:

Business report

Skill	Weighting	Description
Knowledge	8	How well you know meanings, theories and ideas
Application	8	How well you can explain benefits, problems, calculations, situations
Analysis	8	How well you develop ideas and apply theory and ideas to matters under question
Synthesis	5	How well you structure the answer
Evaluation	11	How well you judge the overall significance of the situation
Total	40	

Essay

Skill	Weighting	Description
Knowledge	8	How well you know meanings, theories and ideas
Application	8	How well you can explain benefits, problems, calculations, situations
Analysis	8	How well you develop ideas and apply theory and ideas to matters under question
Evaluation	16	How well you judge the overall significance of the situation
Total	40	

The skills requirement of a question

Unlike AS units, there is no need to identify the critical words in this paper. Only two questions will be asked and both will require evaluation. In the assessment of higher-level questions requiring evaluation, marks will also be given for other skills. Thus factual knowledge displayed will earn marks for knowledge (content), explanations in context and calculations will be awarded application marks, and use of relevant business theories and/or concepts will earn analysis marks.

Analysis

As the majority of marks in this paper are for analysis and evaluation, it is worth familiarising yourself with these skills to ensure that you have mastered them. Students who fail to analyse generally do so because they have curtailed their argument too quickly. The words and phrases below serve to provide logical links in an argument. By using them you can demonstrate your ability to analyse.

- ...and so...
- ...but in the long run...
- ...which will mean/lead to...
- ...because...

introduction

Evaluation

In order to evaluate, you need to demonstrate judgement and the ability to reach a reasoned conclusion. The following terms will demonstrate to the examiner that this is your intention:

- The most significant...is...because...
- However, ...would also need to be considered because...
- The probable result is...because...

Business reports

Thre are six questions based on the format of the Unit 5W paper in this section, each of which is followed by one or two sample answers interspersed with examiner's comments.

Questions

The examination is 90 minutes long. You will be required to write one compulsory business report concerning a decision or business problem based on a set of information provided, and one essay question (from a choice of four).

Both questions carry 40 marks and are equally weighted. Because it will be necessary to spend some time reading the data provided for the business report, you are advised to divide the 90 minutes as follows:

Business report	**45–50 minutes**
Essay	**40–45 minutes**

Tackle the questions in this book to develop your technique, allowing yourself the time indicated above to answer the questions. By considering the specimen answers provided and the examiner's comments, you will be able to see how these questions may be answered effectively and identify (and so avoid) the potential pitfalls.

To help you in applying your learning at the time when the topic is still fresh in your mind, and to avoid delaying the practice of real examination questions, the sample business report questions have been selected in a particular way.

Question 1 is based completely on content from the AS units. This question could be attempted as early as the end of the first year, so that experience can be gained in attempting this style of question. Question 2 is a mix of AS and A2 topics, and is designed to give practice at an early stage of the A2 course.

The remaining business report questions are designed to incorporate material largely on the A2 specification but, depending on the order of planning of the course, it should be possible to answer questions 3 and 6 during the early part of the second year. Students are advised to leave questions 4 and 5 until the latter part of their course.

The synoptic nature of the essay questions means that ideally they should be attempted towards the end of the course.

Sample answers

Resist the temptation to study the answers before you have attempted the questions. In each case, the first answer (by candidate A) is intended to show the type of response that would earn a grade A on that paper. An A grade does not mean perfection. These answers are intended to show the range of responses that can earn high marks. In business studies it is the quality of the reasoning that is rewarded. Candidate B's answers demonstrate responses that contain other points of interest.

These answers are used to show:

- alternative, correct approaches that can earn high marks
- specific problems and common errors, such as poor time management, lack of clarity, weak or non-existent development of an argument, irrelevance, misinterpretation of the question, and mistaken meanings of terms
- responses that may lack quality in terms of certain skills

Examiner's comments

Examiner's comments are preceded by the icon **e**. They are interspersed in the answers and indicate where credit is due. In the weaker answers, they also point out areas for improvement, specific problems and common errors.

Further guidance

Before tackling the questions you should:

- study the next section, 'How to answer the business report'
- scrutinise the mark scheme on pp. 13–14 — this will allow you to identify how your paper will be assessed

How to answer the business report

Before answering the business report it is vital that you recognise that it is only half of Paper 5. You must leave sufficient time to tackle one of the essays.

(1) Practise time management
Allow 45–50 minutes for the report; this will give you 40–45 minutes for the essay. Practise sample reports within this time constraint to get a feel for what is possible.

(2) Read the question carefully and maintain your focus
The data may have many uses, so be careful what you do with it. Clarify the exact requirements of the question in your mind, and plan your format (e.g. arguments for, arguments against, conclusion).

(3) Refer back to the data
In interpreting information it is useful to mention the occasional figure or comparison to clarify your logic to the examiner. This will guarantee that you are responding to the data, as required. But be careful — students often fall into the habit of merely describing rather than analysing data. Do not simply repeat the information.

(4) Take an overview of the situation
With five appendices to scrutinise, it is essential that you take a broad view. The appendices are like a jigsaw — each element may (or may not) provide you with an insight into the solution. But it is only when they are combined that the full picture can be seen.

(5) Synthesise

Synthesis is the ability to select and distinguish between information that is relevant and useful and that which is marginal or irrelevant. This paper is an alternative to coursework, in which students will be gathering information and then sifting through it in order to use the data which allow them to draw the most meaningful conclusion. You should be doing the same here, as this paper aims to test the same skills. Consequently, do not try to include every piece of information. Be selective!

(6) Build up links between the data

Do not take each appendix in turn. This is unlikely to give a logical structure and, more significantly, it will prevent you from drawing conclusions that rely on links between pieces of information. Identifying that there is some (or even no) correlation between two different appendices will enhance your answer. For example, if Appendix B shows a fall in sales, this might be connected to the price increases shown in Appendix D, or the new competition noted in Appendix A.

(7) Explain and analyse

There is a tendency for students to expect numbers to explain themselves. They don't! Develop your answers fully, so that you can be awarded marks for the higher-level skills. Look at the mark scheme for business reports and ask yourself whether your answers meet the descriptor for level 4 analysis.

(8) Draw a conclusion

The report requires you to make a reasoned decision. Does your structure allow you to provide a recommendation based on evidence?

(9) Don't get bogged down in number crunching

A calculator will be useful, but the paper is devised to limit the number of calculations required. Invariably, numbers such as ratios will already be calculated and included in appendices. Every moment spent calculating reduces the time available for writing. There should be no need to carry out lots of calculations. However, comparisons between data, particularly with respect to identifying trends, will be pertinent.

(10) Write in report format

This is a report and should be presented in a suitable style. But don't bother with elaborate use of numbered paragraphs, headings and sub-headings. A simple report format as shown below will save time:

To: xxxxx
From: vvvv
Date: nnnnn

TITLE OF REPORT
1 Arguments for
2 Arguments against
3 Recommendations

The details should be provided in sections 1 and 2 (more sections can be introduced if appropriate to the argument). The 'recommendations' section can also act as a memory aid to encourage evaluation of the arguments.

Business report mark scheme

Marks awarded per question: **40**

Mark summary

- Knowledge and comprehension   **8 marks**
- Application of knowledge   **8 marks**
- Analysis of evidence   **8 marks**
- Synthesis   **5 marks**
- Evaluation   **11 marks**

Detailed mark scheme

Knowledge and comprehension   **Maximum 8 marks**

LEVEL 3	Includes a range of relevant material fully explained and presented appropriately	6–8 marks
LEVEL 2	Includes explanation of relevant material, which is presented appropriately	3–5 marks
LEVEL 1	Includes some relevant material which is presented appropriately (up to 2 marks for report format)	1–2 marks
LEVEL 0	Includes no relevant material	0 marks

Application of knowledge   **Maximum 8 marks**

LEVEL 3	Relevant data applied in detail to the context of the question and showing critical perspective	6–8 marks
LEVEL 2	Relevant data applied in detail to the context of the question	3–5 marks
LEVEL 1	Relevant data applied to the context of the question	1–2 marks
LEVEL 0	No application of data to the question	0 marks

Analysis of evidence   **Maximum 8 marks**

LEVEL 3	Substantial analysis of the data, identifying key issues and demonstrating insight and depth	6–8 marks
LEVEL 2	Analysis of the data, identifying key issues	3–5 marks
LEVEL 1	Limited analysis of the data presented, showing some understanding	1–2 marks
LEVEL 0	No analysis presented	0 marks

Synthesis   **Maximum 5 marks**

LEVEL 3   The report is well thought through, making it easy to follow   5 marks
          the logic, the communication and the recommendations,
          which draw together the most appropriate evidence and
          arguments

LEVEL 2   The report's structure is well thought through, making   3–4 marks
          it easy to follow the logic, the communication and the
          recommendations

LEVEL 1   The report has a structure and is built into a connected   1–2 marks
          whole

LEVEL 0   The project is unstructured and lacks coherence   0 marks

Evaluation   **Maximum 11 marks**

LEVEL 4   Appropriate conclusions justified by the evidence,   10–11 marks
          showing an awareness of the most relevant underlying
          themes or issues and their potential implications for the
          business concerned

LEVEL 3   Appropriate conclusions justified by the evidence,   7–9 marks
          showing an awareness of the most relevant underlying
          themes or issues

LEVEL 2   Appropriate conclusions which are partially supported   4–6 marks
          by the evidence presented

LEVEL 1   An attempt at drawing conclusions, but based on hearsay   1–3 marks
          or assertion rather than argument based on the evidence

LEVEL 0   No attempt to draw conclusions   0 marks

Nerds, Goblins and Nasties

Background

NGN Ltd commenced trading in 1981, capitalising on the newly developed market for adventure games. Currently it produces three games — Nerds, Goblins and Nasties — with production at three bases in Slough, Leeds and Walsall.

Nigel Northey, its founder, is approaching retirement and profit has fallen recently. The venture capitalists who provided financial support to Northey are concerned that their investment may start to lose money.

They have approached you, as a business consultant, to advise them on how the efficiency of the business can be improved. Your initial research has yielded the data shown in Appendices A to E.

Using the data provided, recommend actions that will enable NGN Ltd to improve its profitability.

Appendix A Market research data

	Nerds	Goblins	Nasties
Annual sales (units)	11,000	18,000	28,000
Size of sample	100	30	60
Sampling method (Q = questionnaire)	Postal Q	In-depth Q	Retail audit
High users (%)	35	20	60
Normal users (%)	40	30	30
Low users (%)	25	50	10

Appendix B Elasticity of demand

	Nerds	Goblins	Nasties
Price elasticity of demand	(−) 3.0	(−) 1.5	(−) 0.5
Income elasticity of demand	+ 0.3	+ 1.0	+ 2.0

Appendix C Factory production

Factory:	Leeds	Walsall	Slough	Total
Production of Nerds (% capacity)	4,000 (67%)	4,000 (50%)	5,000 (56%)	13,000 (57%)
Production of Goblins (% capacity)	4,000 (100%)	5,000 (63%)	9,000 (90%)	18,000 (82%)
Production of Nasties (% capacity)	12,000 (100%)	4,000 (67%)	12,000 (100%)	28,000 (93%)

report

Appendix D Budget information (latest year)

Factory:	Leeds	Walsall	Slough	Total
Budget allocation	£240,000	£150,000	£300,000	£690,000
Actual expenditure	£250,000	£125,000	£280,000	£655,000
Variance	(£10,000)	£25,000	£20,000	£35,000

Appendix E Stock control records

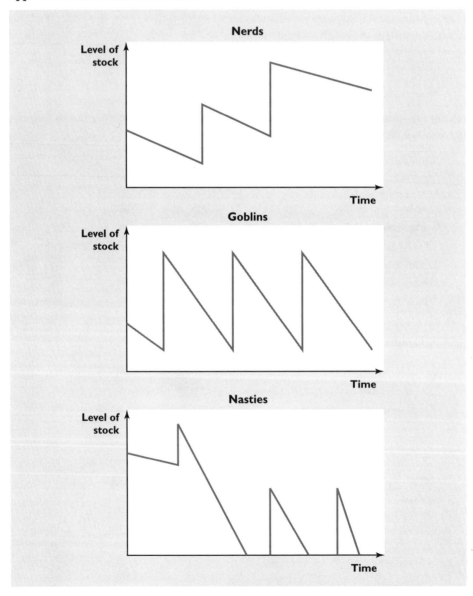

Answer to business report 1: candidate A

To: Mr Venture Capitalist **Date:** dd-mm-yr
From: Candidate A

Title: WAYS TO IMPROVE THE PROFITABILITY OF NGN LTD

1 Findings

1.1 Market research has shown that there are areas for improvement in the firm. The market research shows that the product is popular with the general public.

1.2 One of the main causes of concern is the Nerds game. Only 11,000 units were made last year, which did not generate much profit. The product is still very well received though — 75% of people questioned were high or normal users. This means that there is scope for improving this poor sales figure, because people have a basic interest in the product.

> 🖉 Although there is some validity in this claim, it is an assumption to indicate that it does not make profit. With low costs it might be the most profitable game. The final sentence shows a sound interpretation of the market research data. Although this type of research is based on opinion rather than fact, its usefulness to a firm should not be overlooked. These types of data are often underused in numerical analysis, but they can provide useful insights as shown here.

1.3 The income elasticity of the product is +0.3. This means that there is an interest in the product, and sales could be targeted at people with higher incomes.

> 🖉 Concepts such as income elasticity of demand are often underused. In this case there is some attempt to use it, but the relatively low value of income elasticity does not support the conclusion offered.

1.4 The company has the capabilities to produce more Nerds if sales increase, so the costs of extra production are not likely to be an issue. Nerds are produced to only 57% of capacity, so this would be easy to increase. There is also a fairly large level of Nerds in stock already, so the company would be prepared for extra sales without any extra fixed costs.

> 🖉 It is becoming evident that the candidate is focusing on each product in turn in order to draw up a picture and make recommendations. This is a valid approach, but caution must be exercised in case there are generic strategies that are either omitted or repeated three times. An introduction that outlined the structure of the answer would have helped.
>
> Paragraph 1.4 is very good, linking the capacity information to the stock control in order to make pertinent observations and a relevant recommendation.

1.5 Increasing sales of Nerds would be one of the best options due to the simplicity of achieving this and the limited costs involved. However, there are other options.

> 🖉 A simple but effective evaluative summary.

1.6 Goblins is not as popular as Nerds or Nasties according to the results of the in-depth questionnaire. It has an income elasticity of +1.0, however, which could lead to an increase in the popularity of the product. The stock levels decrease very sharply in a short space of time. People may not be able to purchase the product and therefore may lose interest and buy another game. If the levels of stock are at a more constant level, then Goblins can be bought by the customers interested in it, attracted possibly by a new advertising campaign.

> The candidate is now discussing a second product. Again, there is an effective integration of information from different sources, allowing a more rounded view to be presented. (Where possible it is best to combine information from different appendices, but this should only be done if there is a natural connection.) The argument on income elasticity needs to be stated more explicitly (the examiner cannot be expected to interpret what you are thinking), but overall this is an example of excellent analysis.

1.7 A more drastic approach may be to lower prices in a promotional offer to attract customers. The price elasticity of demand for all products is susceptible to changes. A drop in price combined with advertising may boost sales considerably. Although the decrease in price would decrease the profit margin slightly, more sales at a slightly lower price are likely to be more favourable than fewer at a higher price. This offer may also attract more customers, who might buy the other games after the promotion too.

> In sharp contrast to the previous paragraph, this is too general and sweeping. There is precise information on elasticity of demand that could be used to show when a change in price is ideal. However, the observation on the impact on profit margins shows sound judgement, and the last sentence is evidence that the candidate is really thinking of the possible wider implications for the business.

1.8 Budgetary control could be improved too. Leeds could benchmark against Walsall to reduce their waste or learn how to control expenses. However, Walsall is not producing at very high capacity. If they are keeping to budget because of their low production then they may not be very efficient, but it looks as if their budget allocation is very low and so this has been allowed for. On the whole, the variances are favourable and so this is not the best place to find improvement.

> Although the final sentence appears to negate the purpose of this paragraph, by making a recommendation it shows strength if all relevant issues have been considered. Overall, this paragraph is helping to steer the business towards the best course of action. The comment at the end is a reasoned judgement that relates to the question set.

1.9 Finally, an option for increasing efficiency and profitability is to increase profit margins. If the products can be produced more efficiently and more in line with demand, then the firm will benefit. Walsall does not produce amounts near its capacity, and so this factory could be targeted as the factory to make the extra products if sales increase. This would improve economies of scale and save the company money in the future.

> _e_ Having identified individual strategies, candidate A uses this paragraph to illustrate a more general, but very useful, strategy. It confirms the impression that the candidate has recognised the situation facing NGN, and is able to use an understanding of business studies to make appropriate recommendations.

2 Conclusions and recommendations

2.1 The company certainly has a future in the industry; research shows a clear interest from the public in the products offered.

2.2 The best option would be to concentrate on the advertising of these products. The benefits will have to be weighed against the cost of advertising though. Marketing needs to be effective, and therefore is going to be expensive. Can the company afford the cost? If so, this is the best option available.

2.3 A slight reduction in price would also be effective, but this depends on the financial position of the company which is not given. If profits are falling, and there is a lack of available funds, then this type of strategy may be too risky.

2.4 Improving efficiency would be a good strategy, but it would be important for workers to accept the implications of this policy.

2.5 Overall, money will need to be spent on increasing sales. The market and the spare capacity are both there; a step-by-step plan to coordinate advertising and production should increase efficiency and profitability.

> _e_ This conclusion shows good technique. It is difficult to avoid some repetition if a conclusion is presented, but virtually every comment is extended by a further insight that indicates the factors that should be considered. For example, the conclusion on marketing is qualified by the recognition that the financial position needs to be satisfactory; changes in production may need the workers' support, and the need to coordinate production and advertising is a mature observation.

> _e_ **This is a high-quality grade-A answer. Candidate A has shown an excellent understanding of the topics drawn upon, which has led to valid, well-supported recommendations. The fact that there is a rather generalised treatment of some information, and that there is very little on Goblins and Nasties, does not detract from an answer that shows an excellent understanding of the issues. There are a lot of data in this particular case, and it would be unreasonable to expect a 45-minute answer to include every possible observation. The skill of selecting relevant data is a key element of the business report and has been demonstrated well in this answer.**

■ ■ ■

Answer to business report 1: candidate B

To: NGN Ltd   **Date:** dd-mm-yr
From: Candidate B   **Ref:** NGN1

Re: IMPROVING PROFITABILITY OF NGN LTD

The market research information has shown that the product Nasties has the highest annual sales of 28,000 units. However, the information also shows areas where NGN Ltd should change and improve departments in the company.

🖉 This is too vague. No attempt is made to justify the second sentence.

The company used different size samples and methods of sampling to find that the highest percentage of high users buy Nasties. However, the highest percentage of normal users buy Nerds. With the percentage of low users categorised, it shows a high 75% preferring Nerds or Goblins rather than Nasties.

🖉 This is too descriptive. The purpose of numeric data or tables of information is to simplify the presentation of data. Only describe data when it is needed as evidence to support an argument.

The information for the elasticity of demand shows that Nerds' price elasticity is higher than the other products at –3.0 in comparison to Nasties which has a very much lower –0.5. The income elasticity figure shows that Goblins and Nasties are more susceptible to changes in income as they are higher and that they are likely to appeal more to high-income earners.

🖉 An up-and-down paragraph. It starts descriptively, but then income elasticity is neatly explained. Unfortunately, the full logic is not developed. This is a missed opportunity to present a coherent strategy on how the firm should plan for changes in consumers' incomes or target certain income brackets.

The factory production figures show that the production of Nerds in all three factories is not making the company very efficient, as it is far from full capacity at 57%. However, the production of Goblins is much better generally in the three factories, although Walsall could be improved.

The budget information shows that Leeds is the least efficient factory and Walsall is the best with a favourable variance. Overall, the budget variances are favourable which is good for the company as a whole.

In addition, the stock control records show that Goblins' history is steady and predictable. It has peaks and troughs and yet never runs out completely, which is good organisation. The other products are the opposite — very unpredictable with the stock actually running out at a couple of points.

🖉 These paragraphs are rather frustrating. The candidate is demonstrating a very good understanding of what the data signify, but is not using it to make recommendations. Finalising an argument is a fairly simple step, but one that needs to be taken.

Recommendations

It is very difficult to decide which product is actually having a substantial impact on the company's efficiency and therefore profitability, which is why an eclectic approach must be taken to improve the company. In order to improve the profitability of NGN I recommend that to begin with more market research is done to clarify which markets want which products. The samples were different sizes and so their reliability is questionable and different methods of sampling could make any comparison unfair.

🖉 The ideas presented in this paragraph are valid, but at this stage of the answer they are rather avoiding the main question. Comments on the lack of information and the weaknesses of the data should be used to place a slight warning against the recommendations, rather than becoming the focal point of the answer. Very few business decisions are based on perfect information, but a decision is still needed.

However, from these results I think advertising should be increased for Nasties, which has high annual sales but is only popular with high-income users. I think that its current situation needs to be improved. Sales of Nasties and Goblins would increase much more if they were advertised more heavily to high-income groups.

🖉 This final sentence has filled in the gap identified earlier, as the candidate now shows how to use the income elasticity.

I think that cost control needs to be investigated in Leeds, in order to improve efficiency in the budgeting. This will improve profit by cutting unnecessary costs.

🖉 A valid idea, but a brief reference to Appendix D would have confirmed the reasoning behind this recommendation.

The stock control records show that there always seems to be too much stock of Nerds and the opposite for Nasties. However, as Nerds' elasticity of demand is –3.0 I feel that price cuts could improve its profitability. Nasties could improve profitability by increasing its price as its price elasticity of demand is low at –0.5.

🖉 The candidate has now really got into the swing of things and produced two valid strategies, although both should have been explained more fully.

A general increase in awareness and organisation in the company would improve NGN and, as a result of this added effectiveness, its profitability should improve. Each of the products has its own advantages, but they all have disadvantages which need to be minimised for the company to remain successful.

🖉 No real credit has been given here, as the answer is moving away from the data. The time spent on this final part would have been better used developing the previous paragraph. As the answer progressed it became stronger, showing a sound ability to apply business concepts to this particular situation.

🖉 **The breadth, rather than the depth, of the answer was its best quality. Overall, it would be a good C grade.**

B2
business report

Smelly Shoos

Background

Shoos plc is a large manufacturer of pharmaceutical products. Recently it has taken over a small rival, thus acquiring three new brands of perfume: Adelphi, Beautius and Constance. It intends to sell these perfumes alongside its existing range.

In your new role of product manager for these three new brands you have been given the information shown in the attached appendices.

Using your understanding of business and the data provided here, recommend strategies for the future to allow Shoos plc to maximise the benefits from its acquisition of the new brands.

Appendix A Social class of purchasers of perfumes

Social class	% of national population	% of buyers of Adelphi	% of buyers of Beautius	% of buyers of Constance
A	2.8	11.0	2.5	0.2
B	18.6	32.5	14.0	1.1
C1	27.5	37.5	27.7	4.8
C2	22.1	14.2	32.0	35.6
D	17.6	2.9	16.0	29.9
E	11.4	1.9	7.8	28.4
Total	100.0	100.0	100.0	100.0

Appendix B Recent sales of perfumes (units sold)

Brand of perfume	Product sales (000s)		
	2 years ago	Last year	This year
Adelphi	75	85	100
Beautius	510	500	500
Constance	420	410	400

Appendix C Changes in disposable income by social class

Social class	Percentage increase in disposable income per annum		
	Last year	This year	Next year*
A	3.5	3.7	2.4
B	2.9	3.9	1.9
C1	1.8	1.9	3.3
C2	1.4	2.3	3.6
D	0.2	0.2	3.6
E	0.0	0.0	4.8

*Forecast change

Appendix D Economic data

	2 years ago	Last year	This year
Unemployment (%)	8.3	7.5	6.3
Inflation (%)	3.2	2.7	3.5
Wage inflation (%)	4.3	3.2	3.5
Economic growth (%)	2.3	3.0	2.9

Appendix E Financial data for current year

Variable	Adelphi	Beautius	Constance
Selling price per unit	£30.00	£18.00	£10.00
Direct cost per unit	£16.00	£12.00	£8.50
Contribution per unit	£14.00	£6.00	£1.50
Fixed cost per unit (allocation)	£6.00	£3.50	£2.00
Profit per unit	£8.00	£2.40	(£0.50)
Units sold	100,000	500,000	400,000
Total profit for brand	£800,000	£1,200,000	(£200,000)

■ ■ ■

Answer to business report 2: candidate A

To: Managing Director **Date:** dd-mm-yr
From: Product Manager (Candidate A)

Title: STRATEGIES TO ALLOW SHOOS PLC TO MAXIMISE THE BENEFITS FROM THE NEW BRANDS

Findings

The three different perfumes are at different stages of the business cycle. Adelphi seems to be in the growth stage, meaning sales should continue to increase in the future. Beautius seems to be in between the maturity and decline stages, and Constance seems to be in decline, going on the last 3 years' figures.

🖉 A positive start; immediately there is a link between the case and business theory, and the applications are all correct. The final phrase shows judgement in that it acknowledges the difficulties involved in drawing conclusions based on limited data.

From this I think that Shoos plc needs to implement extension strategies for Beautius and Constance. To do this the company should change the products' marketing mixes, for example by boosting advertising expenditure. A more long-term alternative would be to let these products decline, whilst extra money is devoted to research and development to introduce new products. This is more risky as there is no guaranteed return since customers may not buy them, and the goodwill of Beautius and Constance customers will be lost.

 The argument has been extended well, with a relevant example of an extension strategy. The further expansion is also a sound approach, although it is a relief to see that the weakness of replacing the two perfumes is recognised by the candidate. Although the initial long-term proposal is unlikely, it is not inconsistent with the data and so exploration of it as a strategy is perfectly acceptable. However, tactically it is usually better to stick to a more narrow focus to avoid the chance of irrelevance.

If the extrapolations for next year's 'percentage increase in disposable income per annum' prove to be correct, it might give Shoos plc ideas for extension strategies. The main social classes that will be gaining most disposable income are classes C2, D and E. This could mean that advertising to catch these markets will be an advisable extension strategy, as long as this won't ruin any image the perfumes already have. The data show that Beautius and Constance especially are those perfumes that already sell to the aforementioned social classes. This means that specially targeted advertising is a reasonable strategy for any excess spending in this area.

 Excellent! This is a very focused response, and yet it is still extending the original logic. The relationship between the social class and the type of extension strategy is very shrewd, and would be credited accordingly.

From the economic data only the unemployment figures appear to be stable enough for extrapolation. It appears that unemployment will continue to fall, which is good for all manufacturers as the population has more money to spend because the newly employed receive more income. Sales increases, safer jobs and more disposable income for everyone follow on from this. Therefore sales should increase or at least maintain stability for Shoos plc in the future.

 The investigation of the impact of falling unemployment is justified in the initial statement, and the logic displayed is excellent. Examining the possible impact of unemployment on different social classes and the consequent effect on each perfume could have provided a further insight. The skill of synthesis is demonstrated by the candidate giving the reason for not using the other data.

The financial data for the perfume brands are very interesting. Constance is losing money. However, it is contributing £600,000 to fixed costs, so rather than scrapping production altogether I believe the implementation of leaner production methods would be a better alternative. Rationalisation with tight budgetary constraints could make the whole business less wasteful and therefore more profitable. Based on this financial data I would advise Shoos not to radically change Adelphi and Beautius, as they are very profitable. Even if sales do not increase (the future increases in disposable income will help the lower classes more) next year, they should make a lot of profit if they are left alone.

📝 This is a very mature piece of analysis and evaluation. It is always worth distinguishing between contribution and profit in situations where a product is allocated certain fixed costs. The recognition that Constance has a role is critical in this case. Although the movement into lean production is not directly related to the numerical information provided, the candidate has introduced it in a way that makes it a relevant factor for investigation. The latter part is also very good. When asked to make a decision, it is often tempting to hunt down reasons for change. This candidate has recognised that radical change is not required for Shoos.

Alternatively, increasing spending on R&D will potentially bring in new brands to replace these current brands. It depends on Shoos plc's history. It appears that it has had problems producing or launching brands; otherwise it probably wouldn't have bought the company that made these three perfumes.

📝 There is no proof of this, but equally it is perfectly feasible and therefore a logical conclusion that would be credited.

Conclusion

I recommend that Shoos plc uses extension strategies on Beautius and Constance, targeting the lower social classes with advertising campaigns, increased distribution, and maybe a lower price if the product's price elasticity of demand would allow for it. I would not change Adelphi as the existing strategies are working well, and its high price could be damaged if Shoos tried to make it appeal to a wider range of social classes.

📝 Largely repetitious but neatly draws together the arguments presented earlier. The comment on the price elasticity of demand adds value to the answer.

Also, rationalisation and lean production could make all three products more profitable. Examples include just-in-time production or kaizen/continuous improvement. This should maximise efficiency and profitability. However, the company objectives should be considered to avoid a strategy that causes conflict with another objective.

📝 The final paragraph is less relevant and too generalised. The potential conflict with other objectives is often a valid line of argument, as the desirability of an action often depends on what one is hoping to achieve. However, in this case there is no suggestion of what the objectives might be and the possible conflict that could be caused, and so no credit would be given for this point.

📝 **Candidate A has produced a mature and well-judged response. The selection of information is excellent and the logic behind this selection is well demonstrated. The answers have been continually applied to Shoos plc and have used good business principles in reaching conclusions. This would be a high grade-A answer.**

■ ■ ■

Answer to business report 2: candidate B

To: Shoos plc   **Date:** dd-mm-yr
From: Product manager

Subject: STRATEGIES FOR MAXIMISING BENEFITS

Looking at the data, I would say that a marketing campaign or a revamp of the brand Constance would be a good thing. I think Constance contributes to a large proportion of the company's sales and so just scrapping the brand would be bad business practice. A marketing campaign that could increase sales in the lower-class sector that is most popular for Constance would mean that this perfume could take advantage of the forecast increase in disposable income of lower-class people. This is a very feasible idea as something needs to be done to turn around flagging sales and change the way this particular brand contributes to profits. The tables show an increase in real disposable income for these classes (unless inflation is predicted to rise above this year's figure).

> The opening sentence goes straight into the question, with no introductory comments. In a real business report this would not be good practice, but under examination conditions it avoids any costly waste of time. This may lack a certain style but it is not a bad approach, as long as you have planned the way in which you intend to deal with the question.

> The second sentence is rather vague. Many business studies terms are taken from everyday language, so the use of language needs to be precise. The phrase 'contributes to…sales' is ambiguous — 'contributes to fixed costs or profit' would have been a much more potent phrase. As it is, this does not seem to relate to the business meaning of 'contribution' and so would not be rewarded. (Although the penultimate sentence of this paragraph does suggest that the candidate understands the term 'contribution', it is not being used correctly here.)

> This is then followed by a very useful insight into the market segment. Note how the phrasing of the sentence addresses the question whilst providing a thorough explanation of the data. The final argument is both analytical and judgemental. The breadth of points made ensure that this is a positive start.

Another strategy I would recommend is to try to increase the sales of the brand Adelphi. This is because the sales have increased considerably in recent years. Also it is the most profitable product of the three and still has only had 100,000 sales volume overall. Increasing the sales of Adelphi could be achieved by maybe reducing the price a little bit and making it appeal to the whole population rather than just certain classes. Keeping the brands profitable is most important and this brand has the most potential.

> The logic is less clear, and the dilemma between higher sales or higher profit margin is avoided somewhat. Certain statements (such as the potential of the brand) need to be justified. If this conclusion was derived from the data, then the candidate should have explained how.

Of the three brands, Constance is the only one that makes a loss rather than a profit per unit. I think the direct costs need to be reduced to help the brand to contribute to profits overall. A way to do this could be to relocate in an area with cheaper labour — this would reduce direct costs and increase contribution, benefiting from the brand's high volume. Although it may reduce the quality of the product, the company should consider using cheaper raw materials. This would lower direct costs and so increase contribution per unit.

🖉 There is some potential in the opening sentence, but the subsequent development does not show insight — at best, relocating would take years to yield benefits. However, the argument relating to quality shows analysis and evaluation.

Constance has been struggling in recent years, but the data show low income increases for the social classes that make up most of its customers. The forecast for next year predicts a change, with incomes increasing. It is important that Constance is kept alive — adverts to remind people of its existence should be enough. We may need to run promotions for Adelphi which is predicted to lose sales for next year, unless it is changed to appeal to different classes.

🖉 Some repetition here, but the final two sentences indicate that the candidate is thinking strategically.

Recommendations

A marketing or promotional campaign to persuade the lower social classes to spend some of their increased incomes on Constance would be feasible. The fact that Constance is loss-making also suggests that a reduction of direct costs such as wages and raw materials should be targeted.

🖉 The weakness of this answer lies in its omissions rather than its content. There is a lack of reference to the information. A common fault is for answers merely to repeat or describe the data. This answer certainly avoids that issue but, with only one piece of numerical data actually quoted, it is not always clear how the candidate is reaching certain conclusions. All the same, this is a good explanation of appropriate strategies for Constance. Unfortunately, the limited references to Adelphi, and the absence of any mention of Beautius, places a question mark against the quality of the response. If it is genuinely felt that no change should be made (which could be argued for Beautius), then the logic behind this reasoning must be shown to prove to the examiner that it was a reasoned judgement rather than an oversight.

🖉 **The candidate's overall answer is relatively brief and narrow in its focus, but it shows good application, analysis and evaluation in this limited area and would be awarded a grade D.**

business report

Which marketing strategy?

Background

Zoft Drinks Ltd produces health drinks, specialising in supplying small supermarkets and local corner shops in Britain, Holland and Belgium. It makes two main drinks: Wow and Zap.

In order to boost sales the directors have agreed to support a revised marketing strategy for each product. Preliminary research has indicated that Zoft should either (1) reduce price, or (2) run an advertising campaign targeting shops that sell health drinks.

As the sales manager you have been asked by the board to examine these two alternative strategies and to advise it on:
- **the marketing strategy that should be adopted for Wow, and**
- **the marketing strategy that should be adopted for Zap**

(You may recommend the same strategy for the two products or different strategies for each of them.)

The following information is available to help you make your decision.

Appendix A Sales information

	Wow		**Zap**	
	% of sales	**Sales growth per annum (last 5 years)**	**% of sales**	**Sales growth per annum (last 5 years)**
Britain	80	+10	20	+4
Holland	10	+1	40	+25
Belgium	10	+2	40	+25
	100		100	

Appendix B Correlation between advertising and sales revenue

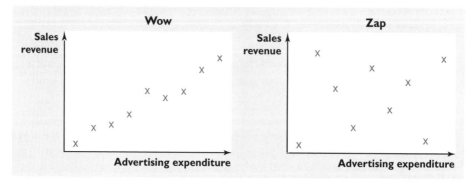

Appendix C Correlation between price and sales

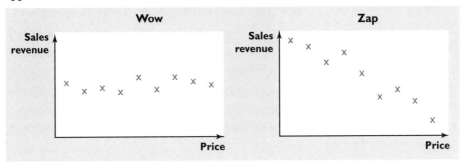

Appendix D Economic forecasts

	This year	Next year	In 2 years' time
Index numbers (base 100 = last year)			
Real disposable income index (Britain)	102	105	110
Real disposable income index (Holland)	102	108	115
Real disposable income index (Belgium)	102	104	107
Exchange rate: £1 = 'x' Euros	1.6	1.55	1.5

Appendix E Market data on Wow, Zap and their main competitors

	Market share (%)			Promotional spending as a % of sales	Average price in euros
	Britain	Holland	Belgium		
Wow	18	9	11	12.3	1.25
Zap	3	24	30	4.4	1.00
Alex	15	40	6	15.0	1.23
Duco	8	12	20	10.1	0.88
Grecco	3	7	30	3.7	0.97
Others	53	8	3	1.6	1.00

■ ■ ■

Answer to business report 3: candidate A

To: The Board
From: Candidate A

Date: Today
Ref: WOWZAP1

THE NEW MARKETING STRATEGY

Introduction

The two products that Zoft Drinks produces appear to be very different. Wow has a much higher price (higher than Zap and also its other competitors). It has a relatively low market share in Holland and Belgium. Although it does not have a high market share in Britain, it is the market leader: Appendix E shows that the British market is much closer to perfect competition than Belgium and Holland.

Zap is much more popular in Holland and Belgium, but does not sell very well in Britain. It has a lower price and this might indicate that price is more important in Holland and Belgium than in Britain.

> These two paragraphs present a predominantly descriptive start, but there is good interpretation of the information here. Although the response is not directly answering the question, it is setting the scene and should provide a foundation for sound analysis.

I shall examine Wow first and make recommendations.

> Unless there are any issues common to both products, this is a sensible approach. Answers to the business report should be structured to suit the demands of the question, and this structure should lead to a relevant answer.

Findings: strategy for Wow

Wow would appear to be an upmarket drink with a high price. It sells well and so I would not recommend a cut in price. Appendix C shows no apparent correlation between price and sales for Wow and so it may even be worth investigating a price increase. I would recommend that this strategy be tested in limited areas to see if the price could be increased even more without affecting sales.

> Very good interpretation has been shown, although statements such as that in the first line are more impressive if the source of the conclusion is stated. The recommendation is logical and the caution shown by the candidate demonstrates judgement, as there is no clear evidence to accept or reject the idea. Linking the price suggestion to the upmarket nature of the drink would have improved this paragraph still further.

Appendix B shows a high positive correlation between advertising spending and sales. Therefore, this is likely to be the best approach to use. Although it is not perfect correlation, there is a very consistent link showing that more advertising expenditure is linked with higher sales revenue. The only possible problem with this conclusion is that it is not proof of a causal link. Some companies set their advertising budgets as a per cent of sales — if so, it is the sales revenue causing the advertising expenditure to rise. However, as the board has asked me to investigate whether there should be an advertising campaign, I do not think this would apply in this case.

> This paragraph is superb. The data are interpreted well, applied to the case, and this leads to a recommendation. This is followed by an excellent observation on the possible lack of causation and is enhanced by reasoning for a possible causal link.

The other product that is heavily advertised is Alex. This has a high price and high sales too and so a natural conclusion is that advertising helps sales and helps to keep the price high. On both counts this will guarantee that Wow makes money for the firm. Incidentally, this strategy might not work in Belgium. All of the market leaders in Belgium sell their drinks for 1 euro or less, and so Wow might have to use a different strategy there.

📝 The justification for the proposal in the previous paragraph is supported by a different source of evidence and logic that points to the same conclusion. The answer is demonstrating a high level of awareness of the company's situation. The observation on Belgium is also a shrewd insight; recognising the need for differing strategies in different markets is a difficult skill.

Sales of Wow have not grown very much in Holland or Belgium and it might be worth investigating the profit that it makes. All the same, it is still the fourth biggest seller in both countries and so I would recommend that it stays.

📝 Although the candidate has not drawn on all of the data, a well-argued set of recommendations for Wow has been produced.

Strategy for Zap

Zap does not sell very well in Britain, although it does represent 20% of its total sales. My advice would be for it to focus more fully on Europe where it is a major seller. In my opinion it would be worth Zoft Drinks looking to specialise, producing Wow in Britain and Zap in Belgium or Holland. This would lead to economies of scale and would cut transport costs. (For health drinks, transport is likely to be a high proportion of the total costs and so cutting these costs might increase the profit by a great deal.)

📝 This paragraph shows the value of building an argument. The relevance of the recommendations arises from the points mentioned at the beginning. Although it is not necessary to draw on personal knowledge in order to achieve an A grade, the candidate's understanding of transport costs would be credited as it enhances the quality of the argument.

Sales in Holland and Belgium have grown enormously in the last 5 years (25% per annum). In Britain Zap has only grown by 4%. By concentrating its marketing effort on the continent, Zap may be able to become the market leader in both countries. If it can become the price leader it will be able to choose the market price. This will mean that it can increase the price and so make more profit. Its low price at the moment will mean that it makes a lower profit than Wow.

📝 There is good logic shown here, although the assumption that Zap's price can be set without any constraints is too simplistic. Without cost data it is also not certain that its profit margin is smaller (although this is probable).

Looking at Appendices B and C, I would recommend a lower price. Advertising does not seem to work for Zap (this might be why the firm does not spend much money on it at the moment). Price rises lead to lower sales revenue (most of the time) and so I would suggest a price cut for Zap (as long as this does not lead to it failing to cover costs and so causing a negative contribution). In Belgium a cut in price to 0.96 euros would make it cheaper than Grecco and should make it the market leader.

report

[?] The integration of the information in Appendices B, C and E has allowed the candidate to produce a well-rounded conclusion. The observation on the reason for the current low level of marketing is particularly good.

Conclusion

The economic forecasts show steady growth, although Holland will be the best market for growth in the near future. The fall in the exchange rate will also make sales in Holland and Belgium more profitable.

[?] More could have been made of this, but the previous comments are so good that this would not affect the overall impression of the answer.

For Wow I would recommend an increase in advertising expenditure (to match Alex), funded by a slight price increase (after some market research). For Zap I would concentrate on Belgium and Holland, cutting the price now (but possibly increasing it again if we become the market leader). The fall in exchange rate will allow us to cut the price in Holland and Belgium by 6% without affecting our profit margins.

[?] Well-qualified conclusions. It should not be necessary to undertake too many calculations, and so the comment on the impact of the exchange rate would have been credited. However, the correct calculation does provide the icing on the cake.

[?] **It is difficult to conceive of a much better answer to this question. Some data have not been utilised, but the purpose of the report is to select the most relevant information. Every argument is presented logically and then qualified. This report would be awarded at the top of the A-grade mark range.**

■ ■ ■

Answer to business report 3: candidate B

To: Board of Directors, Zoft Drinks plc   **Date:** dd-mm-yr
From: Candidate B

Title: MARKETING STRATEGY

Findings

[?] What follows is an object lesson in how not to approach a business report. Candidate B has taken each appendix in turn, and tried to show its meaning. This does not help to respond directly to the question which focuses on the needs of Wow and Zap, as it is not selecting the data that are of particular relevance. Furthermore, in many (but not all) business reports, the strongest analysis is derived from connecting different pieces of data in order to come up with a recommendation. An approach that merely looks at each appendix in turn will discourage the reader from trying to identify these links, and therefore limit the quality of the answer.

Appendix A shows that Wow has 80% of the British market, with Zap having 20%. In Holland and Belgium Wow has 10% and Zap has 40%.

Appendix A also shows that Wow has grown much faster in Britain. It needs to target Holland and Belgium more. Zap has neglected Britain — the British market is much bigger than Holland and Belgium and so it should advertise more heavily in Britain.

✐ There is some relevance to the ideas presented, but the key recommendation is based more on general knowledge than on the data provided.

Appendix B shows the correlation between advertising and sales. These diagrams show that Zoft Drinks should advertise to increase sales.

Appendix C shows the correlation between price and sales revenue. The diagrams show that Zoft Drinks should change price in order to increase sales.

✐ The actual contents of the graphs do not support these conclusions. By talking in such general terms the examiner cannot conclude that candidate B has understood the data. A closer reference to the data might have revealed that Wow would benefit from advertising (but this was not argued by the candidate).

Appendix D shows the increases in real disposable income. All four countries have the same real disposable income this year. This means that living standards are exactly the same level. As Britain is a rich country it means that all three countries can afford health drinks and so Wow and Zap will sell well. Incomes will increase more in Holland and so they should try to sell more there.

✐ The opening sentence shows a misunderstanding of the use of index numbers — the table shows the percentage changes in real disposable income rather than the absolute levels of income for the different countries. However, the observation on the connection between wealth and health drink purchase is valid. This will be credited and any doubts about the source of this idea would be ignored. The final sentence produces a good conclusion — it may be an obvious point but it must still be stated in order to earn marks.

Appendix E shows market shares. Wow is doing well in Britain but needs to advertise more in Holland and Belgium. Zap is equal first in Belgium. If it linked up with Grecco they could become a monopoly. It needs to increase its sales in Britain or it will be pushed out of the market.

✐ This is a rather disjointed set of points. Although Appendix B implies that advertising Wow might increase its sales in Holland and Belgium, the candidate does not explain how he or she reached this conclusion and so cannot be rewarded fully.

Both Wow and Zap must increase their promotional spending. Wow spends the second most and so I would recommend that it increases its spending up to at least 15% so that it matches Alex. Zap does not spend anywhere near enough on promotional spending as a percentage of sales. It should increase this figure up to the level of Wow. Zoft Drinks does not seem to have been very fair to Zap.

✐ The logic is rather simplistic and questionable, but not without some merit.

Wow is the most expensive drink. The cheapest drink is Duco and so they should cut their prices in order to stop Duco taking away all of their sales.

e The candidate is not showing any real judgement — if price was the way to secure sales, then Appendix E would not show high sales for Wow and Zap. To an extent the data are being ignored. The candidate reaches simple, analytical conclusions (but ones that are not supported by the data in this market).

In conclusion I would recommend that big advertising campaigns are run for both Wow and Zap. Their prices should be cut too, although Zap will not need to be cut by so much as Wow.

e The absence of any recognition that these approaches would incur costs considerably weakens the quality of this argument.

e **The candidate has not attempted to integrate the data. More significantly, suggestions have been based on hearsay rather than on the evidence provided. The lack of critical analysis makes this a weak answer. For example, the correlation graphs are assumed to demonstrate correlation, whereas scrutiny of the data shows that this is not necessarily the case. There is some validity in the ideas presented, but this would be a U-grade response.**

Which supplier?

Background

Whyte Goods plc is a manufacturer of kitchen products. One of its major suppliers of components is experiencing financial difficulties and this has reduced its reliability. Consequently, Whyte Goods plc is seeking a new supplier to provide it with £10 million of components per annum.

A benchmarking exercise has been conducted on two possible suppliers of components: Avenue Metals plc and YLN plc.

Using the data provided, recommend whether Whyte Goods should use Avenue Metals or YLN to supply it with components in the future.

Appendix A Financial comparison

	Avenue Metals	YLN
Return on capital employed (%)	25.1	17.9
Acid test ratio	2.8 : 1	0.7 : 1
Gearing (%)	30	55
Average age of debtors	25 days	65 days
Rate of stock turnover	125	18

Appendix B Distribution

	Avenue Metals	YLN
Average delivery charge (index)	100	60
Lead time	2 days	3.5 hours
Distance from Whyte Goods	50 miles	2 miles
Deliveries made on time (%)	99	97

Appendix C Production details

	Avenue Metals	YLN
Total capacity (£m)	100	40
Current production level (£m)	90	26
Capacity utilisation (%)	90	65
Whyte Goods order as a % of capacity	10	25
Capacity utilisation, with WG order (%)	100	90
Productivity (units per head)	70	60

Appendix D Social audit

	Avenue Metals	YLN
Materials bought from less developed countries (%)	30	20
Materials bought from countries with poor human rights (%)	10	0
Materials that can be recycled (%)	85	70
Accidents per 1,000 workers (per annum)	0.3	0.8
Workforce 'satisfied with employer' (%)	55	80
Pollution index (100 = industry average)	60	110

Appendix E Quality measures

	Avenue Metals	YLN
Scrap rate (%)	0.9	0.2
Customers declared 'satisfied' (%)	89	95
Customers who have stopped ordering in the last year (%)	3	4

■ ■ ■

Answer to business report 4: candidate A

To: Managing Director   **Date:** dd-mm-yr
From: Candidate A

Title: RECOMMENDATION OF NEW SUPPLIER

Findings

Having compared the two suppliers I would recommend that we use Avenue Metals PLC.

> 🄴 This would not be recognised as evaluation, as the recommendation is not supported by any evidence. It also raises the question: is the candidate going to try to prove a particular point? If this is the case it may, in effect, halve the amount of data that can be used. The ideal approach is to plan the structure of the answer but only draw up a final recommendation at the end, when the balance of the arguments will be much clearer.

Our current supplier is experiencing financial difficulties and this has led to reliability problems. In our line of business it is absolutely essential that supplies are delivered on time, and this cannot be guaranteed if a supplier is having financial difficulties. If our supplier is unable to buy materials, it may, in turn, be unable to supply us.

🖉 Although the appendices provide most of the data, there will be information contained in the introductory sentences that should be read carefully in order to understand the situation. Candidate A has cleverly used the information to enhance an argument (emphasising the need for prompt delivery for its line of business, and indicating the importance of avoiding a firm in financial difficulty).

YLN plc is vulnerable financially, in my opinion. Its return on capital employed is disappointing and this could lead to financial difficulties in the future. The economy is in a good state at the moment — in a recession YLN could have problems, especially as kitchen products are not purchased so much in a recession and so YLN's customers (such as ourselves) might cut back on orders.

🖉 17.9% return on capital is not as bad as the candidate suggests. Do not exaggerate problems (or benefits). It would be enough to conclude that Avenue is stronger than YLN on this factor. There is a suggestion that the candidate is trying to prove a case, and this can lead to distorted analysis. In a question that requires judgement, you should play the role of the judge, not the prosecuting counsel. However, this does not detract from the argument that is then developed — this is a factor that counts against YLN and has been recognised by the candidate.

YLN is already only working at 65% capacity. If there is a downturn, this figure will fall even more, worsening its efficiency. It is already less productive than Avenue Metals which produces 70 units per head (in comparison to 60 units per head for YLN).

🖉 A closer scrutiny of the capacity utilisation figures might have produced a different conclusion, but the ideas raised here are logically argued and would be credited. Sometimes there is more than one logical conclusion that can be derived from certain information.

Avenue is also more efficient financially in other ways. It has very high liquidity. YLN's ratio is only 0.7 : 1 — this is below the recommended level and could mean cash flow problems for YLN. It has higher gearing (55% of its capital is borrowed and this could cause problems if profits fell or interest rates rose). It is also much less efficient in chasing up its debtors and controlling its stock (these inefficiencies may be causing its liquidity problem).

🖉 Excellent analysis of gearing and liquidity. This would have been improved by a comparison with Avenue's gearing, debtors and stock control.

Avenue is a more socially responsible organisation than YLN, and this will help us to satisfy our stakeholders who place a high value on our social objectives.

🖉 The candidate has 'invented' socially responsible stakeholders. Is this appropriate? Such an approach should be used with caution. The examiner would need to be happy that this was a reasonable assumption rather than an extreme view. In this case, I would consider this to be fair, especially as it is not being accompanied by a series of questionable assumptions. After all, the significance of social audits does depend on the attitude of stakeholders.

4

report

Buying supplies from Avenue will help our firm to create jobs in less developed countries. Our recycling targets will also be helped as Avenue uses far more materials that can be recycled. The lower accident rate at Avenue shows a socially responsible employer, looking after the welfare of its workforce. We will even be helping the environment as pollution control is much better at Avenue Metals.

Although the candidate has selectively avoided the data that favour YLN, these arguments have been supported well.

Social responsibility will become an ever more important issue for firms in the twenty-first century, and so this should be an important factor in our decision-making. However, we may want to discuss the materials that they buy from countries with poor human rights records to make sure that we are not supplied with components that originated in those countries. If our order equals 10% of their total sales we could be in a strong bargaining position on this point.

An excellent qualification of the previous paragraph, improved further by the recognition of the negative aspect of the Avenue social audit.

Avenue's distribution is not as good as YLN's, but this is to be expected of a company that is much further away. The delivery charge is higher, but this is only a small part of the cost — it would be useful to have a cost comparison to help the decision. With its higher productivity I would expect Avenue to be able to offer a lower price to compensate for this. Although the lead time is longer, this is not a problem as we will be able to plan our production more than 2 days in advance, and Avenue is very reliable on deliveries.

Good logical arguments, despite the fact that it is now abundantly clear that candidate A is not being totally objective.

On quality there is very little to separate the two suppliers. Only 3% of Avenue's customers have stopped ordering in the last year (and this may be due to other factors) and it has a high level of customer satisfaction and low scrap rates. Avenue has the spare capacity to supply our order and so I would recommend this supplier, although I would like to compare the prices that it would charge before making a final decision.

Qualifying a conclusion in this way does show judgement, because the last point is very relevant to the situation.

There is excellent logic in this answer. However, unless there is a clear instruction to support one conclusion, this candidate's approach is best avoided. In trying to prove a case, candidate A is forgoing the opportunity to interpret those elements of the data that do not support the desired conclusion. Fortunately for the candidate, there were many points that suggested that Avenue should be chosen. Consequently, the candidate's answer would still have merited a high-quality A grade.

■ ■ ■

Answer to business report 4: candidate B

To: Managing Director   **Date:** dd-mm-yr
From: Candidate B

Title: NEW SUPPLIER RECOMMENDATION

✐ This response is included to demonstrate that there is not necessarily a 'correct' answer to a particular question. Candidate A gained an A grade by arguing for Avenue Metals. Candidate B's answer will also gain an A grade, although the recommendation is to choose YLN as the supplier. In both cases it is the quality of the arguments that secures the grade. However, be cautious — in some cases the evidence will not be so evenly balanced as in this case and one particular conclusion is likely to be stronger than another.

Findings

The first question to ask is: 'Can the supplier produce enough?' YLN is a much smaller firm than Avenue Metals, but a close look at the production details reveals a different picture. Currently, Avenue Metals has an ideal capacity utilisation of 90%, but if it became our supplier this would increase to 100%. This may seem to be efficient but it gives it no flexibility to cope with problems or increases in orders. As a new customer it is unlikely that we would be given preferential treatment and so I would advise against using Avenue Metals. If we cannot get materials, then we stop production.

✐ This paragraph demonstrates a skilled use of the data — projecting the possible future situation rather than concentrating on the present only. There is mature judgement being shown in the final two sentences.

Even without this problem Avenue has a much longer lead time. Waiting 2 days for supplies is much less efficient than YLN, especially if there is a real reason why it may be unable to meet our orders. In contrast, YLN is a much better option. At the moment it has a lot of spare capacity (35%). Our order would bring it up to 90%, increasing its efficiency but still leaving space to cope with sudden changes. Our order would improve its efficiency and we could use this to negotiate a favourable price. Our bargaining position would be strengthened by the fact that our order would equal 25% of its total sales, and so it would work hard to keep us happy.

✐ An unusual approach is being adopted, but the originality of these arguments would impress the examiner, perhaps more than predictable conclusions. The candidate has obviously taken on the role required in the case.

YLN also produces higher-quality goods. Its scrap rate is much lower than Avenue Metals. Although 0.9% is a low figure, it would be a disaster for our company if unsatisfactory components found their way into our products, and so I would argue that YLN will be much more reliable (its scrap rate is a quarter of Avenue Metals' rate). YLN's customer satisfaction is higher too, and this will help to guarantee the quality of our finished products.

> It is often more difficult to cope with very low numbers than with high ones. Whilst at first sight there may not seem to be much difference between 0.2 and 0.9, in the context of scrap rates (which should be very low), the candidate has correctly recognised a significant difference in performance.

YLN is based in the same town and this will allow us to use 'just-in-time' methods. With a delivery time of 3.5 hours we could place orders at short notice, improving our flexibility to our own customers and saving storage space and costs. This would help us to convert some storage space to production space, eliminating waste. If there were any problems, they would be much easier to resolve with a local supplier than with one that is 50 miles away.

> The development beyond the data is not far fetched and is a logical expansion of the argument. The candidate (as with candidate A) is too focused on one side, but is nevertheless continuing to provide sound reasoning.

YLN does not do so well as Avenue Metals financially (this may be because Avenue overcharges its customers?). This may be a weakness of YLN, but is it a weakness that will affect its ability to supply Whyte Goods? In my opinion, as long as the financial analysis shows a secure company, then it should not affect our decision.

> By showing some relative weakness, but then explaining why this is not a serious problem, the candidate is again demonstrating analysis and evaluation.

Looking at the accounts, I do not foresee any problems. Both companies make a good return on capital and so they should be trading in the future. YLN's acid test ratio is low, but close to the minimum acceptable ratio. (If anything, Avenue's is worse as it is much too high, and its excess liquidity is likely to reduce its profitability. It should be buying more fixed assets.) Both gearing ratios are fine. With profitability rates much higher than interest rates, YLN's 55% is an advantage rather than a disadvantage.

> This is better — a direct comparison carries much more weight when trying to assess whether a candidate has weighed up the arguments in order to produce the ideal solution.

YLN does not appear to be very good at controlling its debtors, who take much longer to pay than the debtors of Avenue Metals. However, this may just be company policy — it may give longer credit terms to its customers. This will be to our advantage as we shall be a customer, and it will be better to have 65 days to pay than 25 days.

> A really incisive view. The natural conclusion to draw is that high debtor days means inefficiency, but it is not necessarily the case. In business, few issues are clear cut and the connection to company policy is excellent. The concluding sentence is even better (although a firm should not rely on having a long time to pay if this is poor financial control rather than company policy).

YLN has a lower RST but this means that it will be keeping higher stock levels.

This will mean that it is likely to be more flexible with rush orders and more able to offer a just-in-time supply, as it will have stock already available. An RST of 18 means that it will have 20 days of stock available, whilst Avenue has less than 3 days at any one time.

✐ This is an effective interpretation of the data.

I have not considered the social audit as I do not believe that a business should be held responsible for the actions of other firms. Although YLN is less favourable in this category, pressure groups can target it if they believe there are issues involved. YLN should make its decisions based solely on business criteria.

✐ Although this paragraph might seem to be a 'cop-out', it would not be ignored and limited credit would be given. The final sentence would be considered question-able — social audits would be seen as 'business criteria'.

Conclusions

I would recommend that YLN plc becomes our new supplier. It can produce more quickly and flexibly, is likely to value our custom more, and we will have a stronger bargaining position.

✐ As indicated earlier, this is a grade-A script. Combined with candidate A's answer, these reports present most of the potential arguments that could be produced. However, combining them would leave no time for the essay in the exam!

✐ **It is accepted that there is insufficient time to cover every possible argument, and although both of these candidates excluded (possibly deliberately) a number of potential ideas, this did not prevent them from securing definite A-grade answers.**

Into Europe

Background

Five Star Ltd has enjoyed tremendous success in the United Kingdom, but Cedric Roberts, the chairman, is determined to keep growing, by expanding into Europe. The company provides equipment, advice and technical support for internet users. The firm has built up a large market share in Britain, helped by its particular expertise in providing internet access for mobile telephones. However, to sustain growth it needs to break into the European market, before the competition becomes too entrenched.

As Cedric's most trusted employee, you have been offered the post of managing director of the European operation; but it is possible to enter only one country at this stage. Your task is to prepare a report for Cedric, advising him on which of the four countries listed should be chosen as the initial base for Five Star's European expansion.

Appendix A Internet users in selected countries

	Population (millions)	Internet users (millions)	Internet users as a % of the population
Belgium	10.2	1.8	18
Denmark	5.3	3.0	56
Holland	15.6	3.6	23
Sweden	8.9	4.8	54

Appendix B Mobile telephone use

	Population (millions)	Mobile phone users (millions)	Mobile phone users as a % of the population
Belgium	10.2	3.4	33
Denmark	5.3	3.3	62
Holland	15.6	5.8	37
Sweden	8.9	7.8	88

Appendix C Economic data

	GDP ($ billion)	GDP per head ($ 000s)	Investment (% of GDP)
Belgium	249.3	24.1	20.7
Denmark	174.8	26.3	20.8
Holland	378.3	23.1	20.2
Sweden	228.8	21.2	14.5

Appendix D Employment information

	Belgium	Denmark	Holland	Sweden
Working days lost (per 1,000 employees)	49	41	2	7
Unemployment rate (%)	9.5	5.1	4.0	8.3
Wage rates ($ per hour)	25	30	27	27

Appendix E Competitor information

	Belgium	Denmark	Holland	Sweden
Market share (%) of market leader	13.3	22.9	8.0	33.7
Number of:				
– competitors	40	12	33	6
– competitors with internet-only expertise	30	10	29	2
– competitors with internet and mobile phone expertise	10	2	4	4

■ ■ ■

Answer to business report 5: candidate A

From: Candidate A

Date: dd-mm-yr

To: Mr C. Roberts

Title: FEASIBILITY STUDY INTO EUROPEAN EXPANSION

Introduction

It is vital that we select the right country with care as a mistake could jeopardise future expansion plans (and my career). Therefore, I shall put aside my personal preferences in order to make an objective decision. However, if the criteria used do not produce a clear-cut decision, then subjective factors such as the quality of life for the workforce will be considered as they will be making sacrifices on behalf of the firm by agreeing to relocate.

✍ A rather personalised opening, but it does have the great virtue of putting the candidate into the role of the person in the case. This is an excellent way of helping to keep to the question set. The acknowledgement of 'qualitative' factors is also good, but this is not the ideal place to consider them as there is no real context. It is usually better to incorporate some of the other considerations that might be crucial to the final decision towards the end of the answer, after weighing up the quantitative data.

Findings

Logically, each of the countries listed has similar potential for our services. Both internet and mobile phone usage are increasing and I am assuming that, like television, they will become standard household items. Consequently, my conclusions will be based on potential as well as actual developments. I need to consider actual developments, as it may take too long for the potential to be fulfilled. For this reason I shall make short-term and long-term recommendations. The short-term recommendations will decide the first country to be targeted, but the long-term view will help to decide future expansion.

> ✐ The lack of cross-referencing to the data means that the argument is too vague — the candidate's logic is not apparent. Fortunately, the next paragraph clearly explains the thinking.

All four countries have similar living standards, with GDP per head being highest in Denmark. It is significantly higher than in Sweden which is over $5,000 less per annum. Also, the fact that Sweden invests a much lower percentage of its GDP suggests that there may be a lack of growth in the future, as growth will depend on the level of capital investment (amongst other things). However, these figures apply to the economy in general and so, in themselves, they are not critical, but as the service that we are concerned with is going to appeal to wealthier people, on the whole, this factor cannot be ignored. Minus one point for Sweden!

> ✐ With the exception of the last sentence there is a lot of quality in the ideas pursued here. The candidate is recognising the importance of GDP per head and acknowledging its similarities between most of the countries. In a well-balanced answer this is important (some students have a tendency to omit factors that show little impact on the final decision, and this makes it difficult to assess whether they recognised their potential importance). By including this argument the candidate shows recognition of its importance and identifies that there is little difference between the countries. The combination of GDP and investment has been used to provide a well-reasoned conclusion. The penultimate sentence is excellent — too often there is an assumption that everyone does well in a period of growth and everyone struggles in a recession. The last sentence is intended to provide light relief. However, be careful to avoid any comment that suggests that you are merely adding up pros and cons in order to reach a conclusion. The examiner wants your decision to be based on the relative strengths and importance of the points raised, not the total number of pros and cons.

Internet use is much less developed in Belgium and Holland than in the other two countries. This information could be interpreted in two different ways. Denmark and Sweden are the best markets because the population is more inclined to use the internet. However, in the long term it could be argued that there is more potential for growth in Belgium and Holland. Consequently, they could be a much better proposition in the long term, and if we entered them now they may prove to be less competitive.

> ✐ This is an excellent distinction between the different short-term and long-term consequences.

For our first European venture I would argue that Denmark and Sweden are a safer bet. As service providers we shall have no influence on future growth in the market and it may be many years before the other countries catch up. Also, although on paper there may be no reasons for them not to have the same potential, there may be cultural differences that limit internet use in those countries.

There is real judgement being shown here in the reasons given for the potential high risk in selecting Belgium or Holland.

Another factor to consider is the total population. In this respect, the greatest potential is in Holland (but then again Denmark might be a niche market if everyone aims for the biggest countries).

Mobile telephone use is much higher in Sweden than the other countries, and so our expertise in combining internet and mobile phone technology is likely to be much more useful in Sweden. However, Denmark has 62% of its population using a mobile and so this would be worth targeting too.

Two simple but effective paragraphs. The candidate is using the data well.

Although Denmark has the highest living standards, it also has the highest wage rates and so this might negate some of the benefits. For our type of firm, relying heavily on skilled white-collar workers, I do not think the data on unemployment and working days lost are relevant.

A good point, but it has not been made clear. The candidate is expecting the marker to interpret the thinking.

Looking at the competition does not show a clear picture. There are more competitors in Belgium and Holland, and yet far more users/customers in Sweden. It seems that Belgium and Holland have lots of small firms (the market leader has a low market share too) and so this would make it easy for an experienced firm such as ours to have an immediate impact. The competition will be more experienced and in the form of larger firms in Denmark and Sweden, but the UK is a much bigger market and so this should not be a problem for us.

This is excellent. Under the pressure of an exam, it could be expected that lots of competitors would be seen as the more difficult market situation. However, this candidate has applied understanding of business theory to present a relevant and powerful argument.

Given that we should be using our phone expertise I feel that the bottom row of Appendix E is of most significance. Although Denmark has more competitors, only two of these have expertise in combining internet and mobile phones and so we could provide a valuable service in that country.

Conclusion

On balance I feel that our immediate aim should be to break into the Danish market. Although it has the smallest population, it also has the highest percentage of internet users, combined with high usage of mobile phones. Although it does not match Sweden in this respect, the competition is greater in Sweden, especially in the combination of phones and internet. Denmark has the highest living standards and should be able to afford our services.

✍ This conclusion draws on earlier points but extends them further — good practice.

However, I would see this as a short-term target. Once we have got used to working in Europe I would recommend immediate expansion into Holland (which has a high population and reasonable levels of use, with the potential for growth). It may be possible to use Denmark as the base for this expansion.

✍ This is going beyond the brief of the question and could be deemed to be irrelevant. However, it would be recognised as a qualification of the original recommendation, as it is helping to explain why Holland (despite these advantages) has not been recommended. The key is to make sure that these comments do not become excessive in relation to the central answer.

✍ **This would be a very good grade-A answer. Unlike some business reports, it has been possible to include all of the data in a relevant manner. A particular strength of this answer is the way in which the relative significance of the arguments — showing why a country is being eliminated or why a particular piece of information is seen as less significant than something else — is explained and developed.**

B6

Food for thought

Background

It seemed like an anti-climax for Suki Smith. After 5 years of trying she had, at last, purchased the lease on the local shop. With the number of clubs, pubs and local residents in that part of Oxley, she had always considered it to be an ideal location for a take-away restaurant. The trouble was, she had thought about it for so long that she no longer knew which style of food to serve. She knew that she would offer a delivery service as well as a counter service, but the local Oxley Council bye-laws meant that she could only specialise in one style of food.

As a close personal friend, Suki is asking you to advise her on which type of food she should serve in her takeaway. The results of her market research are contained in the appendices below.

Advise Suki on the style of food that she should sell in her takeaway.

Appendix A Location of the competition

Style of food	Within 1 mile	1–3 miles	3–5 miles	Total
Chinese	1	1	1	3
Fish and chips	0	3	3	6
Indian	0	1	4	5
Pizzas	1	2	3	6

Appendix B Market information (Britain)

Style of food	Visits to a takeaway in last 3 months (% of population)	Deliveries in last 3 months (% of population)
Chinese	44	5
Fish and chips	47	1
Indian	25	10
Pizzas	20	13

Appendix C Market information (Oxley)

Style of food	Market share (%)	Market growth (%) last 5 years
Chinese	28	+ 20
Fish and chips	30	+ 15
Indian	26	+ 30
Pizzas	16	+ 50

Appendix D Investment appraisal

Style of food	Payback (years)	Average rate of return (%)	Net present value (£000)
Chinese	3.6	30	+ 250
Fish and chips	3.0	28	+ 225
Indian	3.5	31	+ 250
Pizzas	2.8	22	+ 155

Appendix E Financial information

	Chinese	Fish and chips	Indian	Pizzas
Average selling price (£)	4.40	3.20	6.75	9.50
Average direct cost (£)	2.00	1.90	4.05	4.25
Contribution per meal (£)	2.40	1.30	2.70	5.25
Gross profit per meal (%)	55	41	40	55

■ ■ ■

Answer to business report 6: candidate A

To: Suki Smith

Date: dd-mm-yr

From: Candidate A

Title: ADVICE ON THE BEST TAKEAWAY RESTAURANT TO OPEN

Findings

I am sure that the takeaway will be a success. With only two other takeaway restaurants within a radius of a mile it is an ideal location, especially given the number of local clubs, pubs and the nearby houses.

Although predictions are always based on estimates, my first inclination will be to look at the profitability of the different restaurants. Your investment appraisal results look promising. It has taken you 5 years to purchase the lease, but whichever type of takeaway you want you will get your money back within 3.6 years. The pizza option has the quickest payback and would be ideal if you want to get your money back quickly, but it is not much better than the fish and chips. Also the pizza store has the lowest ARR% and net present value. This would suggest that in the long run it is not the most profitable choice. It would be useful to know the time period that the investment appraisal covers and the assumptions made. Based on profitability only I would opt for the Chinese or Indian takeaway, but fish and chips may have other advantages.

🖉 This is an excellent opening. The candidate has identified (and explained) the key data to support a conclusion and has then produced a thoughtful analysis of those data. The paragraph also indicates the different circumstances in which a particular option might be chosen. All of the different skills required have been presented in these few lines.

Chinese meals and pizzas have the biggest profit margin but there is no clear indication of the level of sales, and the investment appraisal suggests that there are likely to be different volumes of meals sold since the investment appraisal figures show similar average rates of return.

🖉 An excellent observation. The significant differences in profit margins can be used as the basis of some sound analysis, but this candidate has recognised that profit margins are less meaningful without sales volume figures. Furthermore, a reason has been quoted for casting doubt on the usefulness of this information.

I would advise you to carry out more market research to find out where customers live. If the majority of customers live within 1 mile then it might be best to open up a fish and chip shop or sell Indian food, as there is no competition within a mile. If people travel up to 3 miles this would make the Indian restaurant the best choice, with only one competitor within 3 miles. However, if people are prepared to go 5 miles (or ask for a delivery) then a Chinese restaurant would be the best bet.

🖉 Skilfully presented. Rather than just stating that a conclusion cannot be drawn without this information (a relevant but simplistic view), the candidate has extended the data by showing how further detail could be used to make a decision. This ties the observation of the missing data more closely to the eventual conclusion.

In my experience people would not travel very far and so I would not open up a Chinese restaurant or pizza parlour. In Oxley fish and chips are the most popular, closely followed by Chinese and then Indian. However, the pizza market is growing fastest. How much of a market share is the takeaway going to achieve? There may be new customers who would eat more meals if a new restaurant opened, but my guess is that the new restaurant will just take a share of the existing market. At present there are only three Chinese restaurants sharing 28% of the market (about 9% each). This is much better than the others (the next best would be Indian take-aways with just over 5% each).

🖉 The ability to combine and interpret different sources of information can lead to some powerful arguments. The candidate is showing real insight here in calculating the average market share of each takeaway and using this to show the advantage of opening a Chinese takeaway. However, the same idea could have been presented just by observing that there were fewer Chinese takeaways meeting the needs of a similar number of customers as Indian and fish and chip takeaways.

For this reason I would open a Chinese takeaway, but only if Suki was able to provide the right quality of meals. If her preference for cooking was for fish and chips or Indian, then I think that she should choose one of those options. The data available are incomplete and there is little difference between them. However, it does seem to be profitable, whatever choice is made.

report

I would also look at the market growth. Although pizza sales are growing fastest, there are already six takeaways. This could make a pizza takeaway a 'problem child' — a small market share in a growing market which is attracting new entrants. It might be safer to open a fish and chip shop, as the low growth rate is unlikely to lead to new competition.

This is cautious, but the caution is improving the quality of the answer here.

Weighing up the various factors, I would choose a Chinese takeaway. There are fewer competitors, it has the highest net present value (and a very good ARR%), and the contribution per meal is very good. Furthermore, there has been a steady level of growth that should continue into the future. The major problem that I can see is the location of another Chinese takeaway nearby. However, if Suki offers a delivery service (as indicated), this could become an opportunity rather than a threat. With only one Chinese restaurant 3 to 5 miles away there are probably a lot of people in Oxley who are not very close to a Chinese takeaway. A well-advertised delivery service (it would be cheap to put a flyer in the local free newspaper) could be a major asset.

Base your conclusion on your evidence, as in this answer. The strength of this conclusion lies in the fact that candidate A has made a decision but has demonstrated that it is not an obvious choice. Do not be too firm in your conclusion, unless your evidence suggests there is a clear-cut preferred option. It is very difficult to draw a conclusion without repeating earlier arguments, but the candidate has succeeded in introducing some further developed points here.

This is an excellent response that would have achieved a top grade A. The answer is well rounded, recognising the limitations of the data but still using them to make (qualified) recommendations. Another impressive feature is the reasoning shown for the prioritisation of certain data.

Essay questions

Essay questions

There are six questions in this section. Each question is followed by one or two sample answers interspersed with examiner's comments. If you have not read the introduction to the section on business reports (p. 10), do so now.

What is required for an essay for AQA A-level business studies? Perhaps the best source of advice is the awarding body itself. In 1997 AQA published advice for students on how to tackle essays in the business studies paper. 'The ten golden rules of essay writing' were drawn up to help candidates avoid the main pitfalls. Here they are:

(1) There is no such thing as an essay about a topic
An essay is a response to a specific question, usually worded so that it cannot be answered by repeating paragraphs from notes. Hence, there is no such thing as the 'communications' essay or the 'marketing' essay, because every answer should depend on the question, not the topic. If you have a favourite topic, make sure that the wording of the question is quite clear and that it does not require understanding of more alien concepts before you rush into an answer.

(2) There is no such thing as a one-sided essay
Some questions are deliberately provocative, implying that there is a dominant factor or that it is right to take one course of action. Do not assume that the examiner is asking you to prove it. If there was just one side to an answer, the question would not be worth asking. Usually, the only questions set are ones that can provoke differing viewpoints.

(3) All essays have the same answer
With few exceptions, A-level questions can be answered in two words: 'It depends.' Consequently, the candidate's main task in planning the essay is to consider what the answer depends upon (e.g. the objectives of the organisation, internal or external constraints, culture).

(4) Essays need a structure
When marking essays, it is awful to feel that you have no idea where the answer you are reading is leading. Use the mark scheme as a guide. A logical structure is to present your basic points, explaining and analysing them (using business theories and ideas), culminating in an overall weighing-up of the evidence in order to create a reasoned conclusion that is supported by the evidence.

(5) Most candidates have forgotten the question by their second page
The key to a good essay is the wording of the question. Discipline yourself by referring back to the question regularly. This will be time well spent because it will help you to avoid the cardinal sin of irrelevance.

(6) Every paragraph should answer the question set
A good paragraph is one which answers a specific aspect of the question set in enough depth to impress the reader. It is recommended that you read over your past essays,

asking yourself whether each and every paragraph is directed at the question. You will probably find several that are side-tracks or simple repetition of notes. Do not be tempted to show off irrelevant knowledge; in an examination such paragraphs gain virtually no marks.

(7) Use the content of the question in your answer

Good answers come from the breadth of knowledge and the clarity of understanding the candidate has shown. Generally, if you analyse the question with care you will pick up most of the content in passing. Consequently, a focus on analysis rather than facts will invariably get you the content marks anyway.

(8) You cannot get a decent mark without using analysis

Analysis means using business concepts to answer the questions with precision and depth. The ability to apply business theories and ideas, to break down the question in order to identify the key issues involved, and the use of relevant concepts will all lead to analysis marks being awarded. A word of caution though: do not be tempted to force an idea or theory into your answer. This can lead to irrelevance and wasting time.

(9) Evaluation is the key to really strong essays

With 40% of the marks for an essay being awarded for this skill, evaluation is twice as valuable as any other skill that you can demonstrate. Evaluation means showing judgement. For good marks you need to:

- show the ability to examine arguments critically, and to highlight differing opinions
- distinguish between fact, well-supported argument and opinion
- weigh up the strength of different factors in an argument in order to show which you believe to be the most important and why
- show how the topic fits into the wider business, social, political or economic context

(10) Play the game

Examiners enjoy reading about (relevant) concepts, with appropriate use of ter-minology. They dislike slang or streetwise language (e.g. 'on the fiddle') and any suggestion that the issues are obvious or simple. You should keep your work businesslike and relevant, managing your time to ensure that you can write a thoughtful conclusion.

Essay mark scheme

Marks awarded per question: **40**

Mark summary

- Content   **8 marks**
- Application   **8 marks**
- Analysis   **8 marks**
- Evaluation   **16 marks**

Detailed mark scheme

Content   **Maximum 8 marks**

LEVEL 3	Three or more relevant factors identified	5–8 marks
LEVEL 2	Two relevant factors identified	3–4 marks
LEVEL 1	One relevant factor identified	1–2 marks
LEVEL 0	No relevant points made	0 marks

Application   **Maximum 8 marks**

LEVEL 3	Full explanation of factors	6–8 marks
LEVEL 2	Some explanation of two or more factors	3–5 marks
LEVEL 1	Some explanation of one factor	1–2 marks
LEVEL 0	No application or explanation	0 marks

Analysis   **Maximum 8 marks**

LEVEL 3	Full analysis using theory appropriately and accurately	6–8 marks
LEVEL 2	Analysis with some use of relevant theory	3–5 marks
LEVEL 1	Limited analysis of the question	1–2 marks
LEVEL 0	No analysis present	0 marks

Evaluation   **Maximum 16 marks**

LEVEL 3	Mature judgement shown in arguments and conclusions	11–16 marks
LEVEL 2	Judgement shown in arguments and/or conclusions	5–10 marks
LEVEL 1	Some judgement shown in text or conclusions	1–4 marks
LEVEL 0	No judgement shown	0 marks

Business relocation

Is it right for a business to relocate from Britain to another country in order to benefit from lower wage levels in that country?

Answer to question 1: candidate A

In the global economy firms should be free to make any decision that they wish. With improvements to communication it is much easier for customers and other interested parties to be aware of the actions of companies.

> *e* This is a rather disjointed opening. The first sentence has not been justified and it is difficult to see the direction that the essay is taking. A clear essay plan before starting to write would help the candidate to focus immediately on the needs of the question.

Right and wrong are very subjective ideas and it can be disputed whether this decision is right or wrong in any case. Is it right that British workers are paid much more than people in some other countries? It is hard to justify differentials in pay between countries, and is it fair to ask businesses to right injustices that elected (and non-elected) governments refuse to tackle?

> *e* A good paragraph. Some individuals might query the use of questions on 'right or wrong' in A-level. In fact, the government requires every subject to consider matters of spiritual and ethical guidance in A-level courses. Business studies lends itself fully to the study of such issues and so candidates should be prepared to assess the ethical dimensions of an issue. However, it is important to support individual views with logical reasoning. This paragraph poses questions rather than answering them, and just manages to keep away from an extreme, unsupported viewpoint.

I would argue that the function of a business is to make profit. Any other result is just a by-product. The fact that businesses create wealth and jobs should be seen as a positive consequence of their activities rather than their main purpose.

> *e* A valid idea, appropriately included — but it could have been developed into a much broader argument.

Different countries have opposing views on the definition of right and wrong. It is the government's job to enforce the wishes of society by passing laws that control actions. The business community must not act illegally (e.g. by publishing false accounts) but if there is no law against something then a firm should be allowed to do it. As there is no law to stop firms relocating, they should be allowed to move (as long as they have been through the correct employment law procedures such as consultation and redundancy).

> *e* A well-presented idea delivering an argument and justifying it in a logical manner.

Although the UK might see this as anti-social, it might be seen as a very ethical decision in poorer countries. The Body Shop buys more and more of its supplies from poorer countries. Is this 'right'? Is it taking advantage of low wages? Not according to the Body Shop. It would argue that it is helping the poorer country become richer (trade not aid) and more self-sufficient, so that there will be less chance of it being exploited in the future.

> This is an excellent reference to a real-life company, both addressing the needs of the question and impressing the examiner with the inclusion of a relevant example. Students with some understanding of the activities of the business world are able to draw on their knowledge to enhance or develop their arguments.

It is obvious that whether something is right depends on your viewpoint, and sometimes whether you take a long-term or short-term view. If the business supports the local economy and helps to educate and build the local economy, then I would say that it is right to relocate. However, if it pays low wages, charges the same price and makes huge profits that are paid to rich shareholders, then this would be hard to justify on ethical grounds.

> Mature judgement (evaluation) is being shown in this paragraph. Recognising the context of an action or decision is a critical element of evaluation, as is the comparison between potentially different short-term and long-term consequences.

Relocation decisions are unlikely to be taken on the basis of one factor. Businesses may relocate because their markets are in the low-wage country, or because they are being driven out of business by rival firms which have moved production to lower-wage countries. The textile industry has largely disappeared in Britain because we cannot compete with the labour costs of other countries. However, preventing imports from those countries would be seen as immoral by many people. We would be creating unemployment in those countries.

> Another powerful paragraph, adding to the analytical and evaluative skills demonstrated earlier in the essay. The candidate is showing circumstances in which a particular moral judgement could be made, taking a broad view of the problem. In general, essay questions will be broad in their coverage of the course and so a holistic approach is usually ideal.

Supporters of the free market argue that countries should concentrate on their strengths. If the firm finds that Britain is not its best location then it should be free to move. This will allow Britain to use its resources in a better way (perhaps in firms that require skilled, rather than cheap, labour).

> A nice reference to the free market, recognising that the essay relates implicitly to the desirability of government intervention.

The idea that firms are only interested in profit is outdated. There are many stakeholders in a firm and so the 'right' decision will be the one that meets the needs of as many stakeholders as possible. A decision to relocate is likely to be opposed by many stakeholders — certainly the workers and local community will object as it will reduce the job opportunities locally. Suppliers may find that they will lose sales (but potential suppliers in the new country will welcome the move). Customers may be happy if the price is lower, but there have been examples of customers (Nike, M&S) objecting to firms using cheap labour from other countries.

A well-balanced paragraph, again using real examples to good effect.

In conclusion, it depends on the reasons for the decision and the consequences of the relocation. If there are no long-term benefits for either country, then it could be seen to have not been 'right'. However, Britain has lost many manufacturing jobs in the last two decades without worsening living standards. Although some individuals have suffered from the loss of jobs in industries like textiles, it could be argued that our society has benefited from the removal of restrictions on business decisions. Furthermore, low-wage economies have gained from the new jobs and wealth that has been created.

Mature judgement is being shown here. With 40% of the marks being given for judgement, it is vital that evaluation takes place. Sophisticated arguments will secure an A grade if they are based on accurate content and logic.

The question could be rephrased: 'Is it right to stop a business relocating where and when it wants?' It is hard to imagine Britain without the large number of foreign multinationals that provide jobs in this country. Should we ask companies such as Nissan, Honda and IBM to leave Britain because they are taking advantage of our cheap labour (compared to France and Germany)? Ultimately, society must make its own judgement — people do not have to work for or buy products from unethical firms.

An excellent conclusion is presented, but the last sentence is a teaser offering (but not taking) the opportunity for an interesting evaluation. The notion that consumer sovereignty will make sure that the free market will lead to morally correct decisions is widely used but also widely challenged by opponents of the free market.

It is perhaps unfair to expect a development of this final argument. This is an excellent essay, presenting ideas, applying and analysing them in context, and delivering judgements based on the evidence provided. In essays of this type, candidates can be tempted to produce an opinion that is unsupported (or even contrary to the analysis that they have produced in the essay). This answer would earn a high A grade.

■ ■ ■

Answer to question 1: candidate B

The answer to this question will depend on the circumstances.

This opening line shows some judgement. This is a rather standardised approach, but is nevertheless a useful way of showing evaluation as long as it is supported by evidence and not left as a stand-alone comment. As an opening line there is a probability that there will be no justification provided and so it would be more beneficial to develop this line at a later point.

In a market economy firms will want to locate in the least-cost site. By producing their goods or services as cheaply as possible they will be able to maximise profits, and this is likely to be the main aim of a business. A business must satisfy the needs of its shareholders. If they are not happy, they will sell their shares and this will make it more difficult to raise money for future activities. Also, the shareholders may vote for a new board of directors if they believe that it is not running the company efficiently (and profit will be the main way in which they will measure the success of the company).

Good justification is provided — a nice piece of analysis that clearly establishes the logic for the least-cost site.

This assumes that shareholders want maximum profits. There is a growing awareness that firms should not focus narrowly on the needs of the shareholders (the shareholder concept) but instead look at the interests of all of its stakeholders. (There are also cases where the shareholders do not aim for profit maximising but instead want the firm to look after other factors, such as the environment and ethical matters.) Typically, these stakeholders include customers, suppliers, workers, the government, the local community and managers themselves.

A good contrast to the opening argument. By taking this alternative line, the candidate is establishing the opportunity to produce a weighing up of evidence, leading to the reasoned judgement required in an essay.

There will often be conflict between stakeholders. Customers will want cheap and/or high-quality products, but this will clash with suppliers who want a high price for their products — this would increase the costs (and so the price) for the business. Workers will want high wages and promotion and training. All of these will cost money and this will conflict with the wishes of other stakeholders.

This is an unfortunate development. The answer is now moving off the point — a common error, particularly under examination conditions. Although this paragraph may be seen by the candidate as a logical extension of the previous one, it is no longer addressing the question. The candidate has become distracted by a desire to show understanding of stakeholders' interests, but it is essential that there is no loss of focus. A few minutes spent on a brief essay plan and constant reference back to the title will be time well spent since it will ensure that answers do not drift away from the real task, as has occurred here. Avoid the temptation to show off knowledge just for the sake of it and always remember why you are discussing a particular concept. 'Stakeholders' is a useful concept to show why there may be different views on relocation, but it is not central to this question.

Government will want tax revenue from the firm and so will support any decision that helps the firm to make more profit, but the local community will want wealth to be created. The multiplier effect shows how a local area will benefit from jobs in that area.

Some pressure groups will be pleased if the business relocates, as firms cause pollution. They will be putting waste into the local river, or making smoke that will make the area less pleasant. Depending on the nature of the business, it may also make a lot of noise, lowering house prices in the area. The pressure group will want the business to relocate.

e These two paragraphs confirm the absence of an essay plan. They are not relevant to the question. However, the candidate won't be penalised for this. The examiner is instructed to ignore any irrelevance. The candidate has effectively been penalised anyway by using up valuable time, but no marks are deducted.

There are a number of factors that a business should consider when making a relocation decision. The main ones are:
- the market
- raw materials
- labour supply
- government policy
- transport and communications

e The answer is back on to the topic of location, but only knowledge is shown in this paragraph as none of the points have been explained. As a rule, bullet points are best avoided — the higher-level skills are the hardest to achieve and so an answer should move away from factual statements and on to application, analysis and evaluation as quickly as possible.

In conclusion, the business will find that relocating to a country where wage levels are lower would be the right decision, but only if the other costs — raw materials, transport — are not increased by too much. They will also need to be close to the market. They will succeed if there is a market for the product in the other country.

e A valid but brief conclusion.

e **Despite the poor structure and planning, the candidate makes some relevant points and does provide explanation and judgement. The time wasted could have been used to improve the conclusion that opens up the chance of further evaluation. This response would be worth a C grade.**

Productivity in the UK

A report by McKinsey, the management consultancy group, showed that labour productivity in the United Kingdom was significantly lower than that in the USA, Germany and France. Discuss the possible reasons for the UK's lower levels of labour productivity.

Answer to question 2: candidate A

Labour productivity can be measured in different ways. The most common method is:

$$\frac{\text{output}}{\text{number of employees}}$$

> A good opening. Defining terms used in an essay is always a sensible start and provides a focus for the essay.

However, it is difficult to compare outputs of different countries and so the value of output (rather than volume) is likely to be used.

> A nice insight. Students often accept formulae unquestioningly. This observation is very astute and already the examiner is on the side of the candidate.

A major factor would be the types of goods and services produced. Germany is traditionally skilled at the production of technologically advanced products. These will have a high value, thus increasing the productivity of the workforce. The USA is very skilled at marketing: this increases the price of the products, making the workers more productive (an employee making a pair of Nike trainers will be more productive than an employee making an unknown UK brand).

> A very positive paragraph. The candidate is using general knowledge very effectively in response to the question. Background reading and an awareness of current events are not essential, but it is good to observe a candidate who is using outside information in an essay. Unless used incorrectly, it shows an ability to apply business concepts, one of the key skills required of an A-level student. More significantly, it allows an answer to be placed in context, an essential element of an evaluative answer.

> This should not distract able business studies students though, even if they lack the background understanding indicated by this candidate. A-level business studies is not a test of general knowledge and a student who understands the main concepts will not be prevented from securing an A grade. The key word in the question is 'possible'. This is a question about why productivity in the UK might be lower than the other countries. The paper setter is asking you to use your theoretical understanding of business in order to examine possible causes and then to make a judgement on the relative importance of the ideas suggested. There is no

definitively correct response to this title — after all, if the reasons were known, something could have been done to change matters.

Income elasticity of demand is important here. If a country produces luxury goods (which have high income elasticity), then its sales will increase as the world gets richer. Countries such as Finland have benefited from the growth in mobile phones. The UK is associated with some declining industries and so, as incomes increase, the UK economy does not grow.

🖉 Wherever possible it is advisable to use business terminology. The argument concerns luxury products, but by tying this into the concept of high income elasticity of demand the candidate has strengthened the quality of the answer. Some examples of the declining industries mentioned could have improved the response still further, but this does not detract from the answer overall.

Investment is probably the most important factor. Rich countries can afford to put more money into investment in machinery and technology. This will improve the efficiency of production, making them even richer and more productive.

🖉 The opening sentence is a nice way of leading into evaluation, but only if it is justified. Too often candidates merely offer a sentence like this as their judgement, failing to recognise that evaluation requires a reasoned judgement.

Britain, although not a poor country, does not put so much money into investment, preferring to give higher dividends to shareholders. This short-termism means that our machinery is older and less efficient than that in the other countries, making our productivity fall even further behind.

🖉 Is this true? It reads well and it is a possible factor. Unless there is a clear factual error, the benefit of the doubt will be given to the candidate. A detailed knowledge of worldwide investment is not required, but the ability to recognise the effects of high or low investment is a part of the course. Consequently, this argument would be credited. (The fact that it is correct in comparison to the other three countries is a bonus in this case.) This paragraph also provides supporting evidence for the judgement in the previous paragraph.

Research and development is another reason. The UK has been rather conservative, not wishing to take the risk involved in spending on R&D. As a result, UK firms are less likely to come up with the new inventions that will allow them to reap high rewards. Even where the British have come up with new inventions, they have often been developed in other countries. Ideas such as the hovercraft, computer and helicopter have all been developed in other countries.

🖉 Another excellent paragraph, offering strong analysis and providing more evidence for the final judgement.

The exchange rate has hindered progress. The euro has fallen in value against the pound, making it very hard for UK-based firms to export their products.

question

📝 This adds a further point, but the lack of development means that it will not add any marks to the total. The mark scheme will not require more than three or four separate ideas. Tactically, the best strategy is to move up the levels as quickly as possible. Only introduce further lines of argument if they help you to analyse and evaluate (particularly the latter).

Some people argue that there is a bias against industry in Britain. Top managers prefer to work in the professions (as lawyers or accountants) or in the City, rather than in industry. Financial rewards are much higher in the City, and so few of the most talented individuals are involved in firms that actually manufacture products.

📝 Another paragraph that draws upon the candidate's sound understanding of the business world.

Government policy can have a large impact. Communist countries were not so successful as democracies. This was because there was no incentive for entrepreneurs, innovators or people with high skill levels. Consequently, in these countries industries tended to stagnate. Although Britain has always been a market economy, up until the 1970s there was a lot of government intervention. Since privatisation there has been much more competition. Some of these companies, such as BT, have become much more efficient (with huge redundancy programmes) in order to compete internationally. Even so, they are still struggling to compete. Since many public services have been privatised there have been improvements in productivity and efficiency, as services such as refuse collection have been offered to the lowest tender.

📝 In itself this is another excellent paragraph, but the candidate is beginning to fall into the trap that can snare good candidates. There is a temptation to show that you can draw upon and explain a wide range of suggestions. This should be resisted. This candidate has secured maximum marks already for the lower-level skills, but has not brought the ideas together in order to evaluate fully (although some judgement has been shown so far).

By now candidate A should be drawing to a conclusion. 'Discuss' requires evaluation (in fact all essays will receive 40% of their marks for evaluation) and should not be interpreted as an opportunity for general analysis of a variety of ideas. Whatever the wording of the question, it is safer to draw a conclusion.

The factors that have caused the low productivity in Britain have varied over time and are likely to be different when compared to the other countries mentioned. The UK is less likely to take risks than the USA, and its economy has been restricted more by government intervention.

A lack of investment in new products and R&D will have been significant factors too, as the speed of production will depend on the equipment rather than the worker. Education and training would also be factors, especially when looking at the number of graduates moving into industry.

✏ Some repetition of earlier points, but there are judgements now being made on the significance of different factors.

One common factor is geography. The UK is on the edge of the European market and so would find it difficult to compete with France and Germany, which are more centrally placed. Britain's wealth was partly built on its command of resources, both in the UK and the Commonwealth. With the loss of these cheap resources and the limited land area in comparison to other countries, it is difficult for Britain (with high land prices) to compete.

✏ An excellent conclusion. Introducing a new idea can help if it is an evaluative idea, as here. This was a challenging essay for two reasons: the lack of background understanding might have caused concern, and it is harder to draw a conclusion in an essay that does not lend itself to a 'yes' or 'no' response. Furthermore, specific knowledge would have assisted in making a judgement.

To counter this, it is accepted that there is unlikely to be any widespread agreement on the factors involved. Consequently, a question like this enables you to tailor your answer and play to your strengths, and so produce a convincing response.

✏ **Despite some delay in drawing the answer together, there is evaluation shown throughout this essay. Critical use of phrases such as 'tended to', 'can have', 'are likely to be' demonstrate an awareness of the need to be cautious in drawing conclusions, and in itself this shows that the candidate is exercising judgement. This answer would be awarded a high A grade.**

■ ■ ■

Answer to question 2: candidate B

This is a difficult question to answer without knowing details of the different countries' economies. The USA is a large economy with a huge market, but Germany, France and Britain are all members of an even larger market — the European Union. Labour productivity depends on a number of factors, but the size of the market is an important one.

✏ A nice introduction, indicating a difficulty (evaluative) whilst still offering an opening line of approach.

The size of companies will affect efficiency. If firms are large they can buy in bulk, buy the most technically advanced equipment, employ specialist labour and practise division of labour. As the USA is larger than the UK, this will allow its firms to grow much larger and benefit from these economies of scale.

✏ At first this appears to be irrelevant, with the focus on companies rather than on countries, but it is neatly brought back together in the final sentence. In effect, this sentence has made the earlier part relevant.

Labour productivity will depend on the skills of the workforce. Traditionally, Britain produced cars, ships, coal, textiles and metal products. It has also had strengths in banking, insurance and tourism.

 This is a disjointed paragraph. It appears to be a lead into two different ideas, but neither has been developed.

With changes in the world economy many of these industries have declined. There is now a lower demand for coal and ships, and it has been more expensive to get raw materials in these industries. This would account for the lower levels of productivity. Britain is still efficient in its services, but it is not really possible to measure labour productivity in this type of industry as no product is made. This may be a factor explaining our low productivity, as the statistics may be ignoring the industries in which the United Kingdom is most efficient.

 Better. This is building on the second idea in the previous paragraph (although the first point seems to have been lost). There is some good analysis and application here, with some judgement shown in the final line. Criticism of the reliability of information is a rather 'standard' line, and should not be used to exhaustion, but it is often a very relevant factor and is presented convincingly by this candidate.

The key factor may be the level of skills of the workers. British firms have been reluctant to spend money on training compared to other countries. This means that workers will be less efficient as they will not know the best ways to do their jobs. Education could be a factor too. In the USA there are many more graduates than in European countries. This will help them to understand their jobs more. Also an educated workforce will be able to tackle more skilled jobs, improving the productivity of the workers. Well-trained employees can take more responsibility. This will mean more efficiency. It will also reduce the need for supervision, saving expenses. In recent years, many firms have delayered, improving efficiency as output has stayed the same, but with fewer employees.

 As with candidate A's answer, whether this is a genuine factor could be challenged. However, as before it is not a problem because it is a possible reason. This candidate has argued the case well and would receive good analysis marks here.

An educated workforce is more likely to spot new ways of doing things. This will lead to better production techniques, which will improve efficiency.

Trade union power could be a factor. In British industry there has been a 'them and us' attitude. Even though trade union power has declined recently, for many decades productivity was held back by restrictions imposed by trade unions. These would have made it more difficult to use the most efficient methods. It would be worth seeing recent changes in productivity. Recently Britain has enjoyed economic growth at a time when America had a recession. Thus although this may not be a factor any more, it could have led to Britain being behind other countries and unable to catch up.

🖉 The last three sentences are excellent, showing clarity of thought and a keen awareness of the meaning of the question. Although the argument might have initially appeared to be dated, the final part of the answer makes it relevant and displays judgement.

Motivation could be a problem. The divisions between employees and employers in the UK may have led to workers feeling undervalued. This would have lowered morale and if workers are demotivated they will work less efficiently. This may be due to management methods, as Japanese managers have been more successful in running car manufacturing in Britain than British managers.

To evaluate, I would argue that there is no one dominant factor causing this situation. I would want to examine the details of the survey before drawing a firm conclusion — if services are excluded it may not show a true picture. I would also want to see the extent to which Britain's productivity is lower, and have a comparison with other years. If this shows a narrowing of the gap, then factors such as the trade unions or government intervention could be blamed. If the gap were not narrowing, then I would argue that it would be a longer-term factor such as economies of scale or education and training of the workers. However, although these factors would explain the difference between Britain and the USA, they are unlikely to explain the difference between France and Britain.

🖉 Again, the student's approach to the conclusion may appear to be following a formula, but it does work. By opening the final paragraph in this way, it is more likely that a judgement will be made. Excellent judgement is shown in the section on the gap being narrowed and this would be rewarded accordingly. The final sentence (recognising the weakness of a conclusion) is a judgement too. In isolation this is not ideal, as it is avoiding the issue somewhat, but combined with a positive conclusion it will add quality to an answer by showing that the candidate is aware of limitations in the final reasoning. Overall, this would be another high A grade.

Look back at candidate A's response. Candidate A appeared to have a much better general knowledge and argued on that basis, focusing on types of goods, income elasticity, investment, R&D, business culture and government policy. Candidate B has produced a very different set of responses, capitalising on a talent for logical analysis and understanding and application of business theory. The focus is on economies of scale, labour skills and education, trade union power and motivation. This is a more narrow focus and produces a completely different set of ideas from those of candidate A, but still broadly achieves the same aim.

🖉 **Invariably there is no one 'right' answer to a business studies essay. It is the quality of reasoning that is being assessed and both of these candidates have shown that quality.**

Take-over decisions

Discuss the factors that an electrical retailer would consider in making a decision to take over another business.

Answer to question 3: candidate A

Take-overs can be horizontal, vertical or examples of diversification. A horizontal take-over would involve the buying of a competitor, such as Currys buying Comet. Vertical would mean integration with a supplier or a customer. As the firm in question is a retailer, this would have to be an example of backward vertical integration (taking over a supplier). Diversification means buying a firm in a different line of business.

☑ A good introduction, defining or clarifying many of the terms needed in the essay.

The reasons for the take-over will depend on which of the above applies. Horizontal integration will help a firm to gain control of the market. If the firm can eliminate its competition then it can charge whatever price it likes and so maximise profit. However, in this country the Competition Commission has the power to prevent a take-over if it thinks that this will happen. Recently the Commission has declared that electrical retailing is competitive and so it is probably OK for such a take-over. However, if the new company owned more than 25% of the market it is probable that it would be blocked. Thus the predicted reaction of the Competition Commission is a major factor that would be considered by an electrical retailer.

☑ A strong paragraph, demonstrating both application and analysis, drawing on the candidate's knowledge of both the business world and business theory and concepts. This has allowed an early evaluation of one of the key factors.

Horizontal integration leads to economies of scale — larger companies can buy in bulk, get cheaper loans and so on, helping them to undercut the competition. If price is important to the customers, this could be the major reason for the take-over. However, the retailer must be careful. Many mergers fail because the firm becomes too large, suffering from diseconomies of scale such as poor communication. In general, electrical retailers seem to compete fiercely on price and so a take-over would be a good idea, but not if the firm has a reputation for customer care and individual service — this could be damaged by a take-over.

☑ This paragraph offers further reasoning and good analysis, but the argument has tailed off quickly without really saying why a take-over might damage reputation. Still, there is evaluation shown in the cautious use of language. Over-certainty can be a weakness in an answer, unless the evidence is clear.

Vertical integration could be very useful too. This would guarantee the retailer first choice of supplies. Taking over a manufacturer would improve its ability to offer after-sales-service and to provide specialist products, tailor-made to the customer's specification. This would increase the profit margin. The retailer could use special offers on its own brands to entice more people into the shop.

📝 More analysis, but there is scope for evaluation of these factors. Unfortunately the candidate has not seized the opportunity this time.

Diversification would help to spread risks. At present electrical retailing seems to be profitable, but in a recession sales may drop and so a take-over of a supermarket, for example, would help it to overcome difficulties.

📝 There is a lot left unsaid here. Do not expect the examiner to make up your line of argument for you. Show why a recession would be more of a problem for an electrical retailer than a supermarket and then tie this into the reasons for the take-over.

There are many other factors behind take-overs. The culture of the two firms would need to be merged. A power culture in one firm might not go well with a task culture in the other, and a disunited company could create problems for the new firm.

📝 These brief paragraphs have potential but would not be rewarded as much as a more focused and fully developed line of approach would be.

Sometimes a take-over allows a firm to acquire valuable assets, such as patents or brand names. This is not likely to apply so much to retailers, but if one has obtained good locations then this could be a factor. The government is now making it more difficult to locate in out-of-town centres: a firm might be very keen to buy another business that has a lot of sites that it could not get in any other way.

📝 The opening sentence introduces a thought and then deflates the argument. This is an acceptable way of evaluating as long as some valid points are made and supported. This approach should be treated with caution, but recognising the weaknesses in a policy is an important business skill (though not if you can never identify a worthwhile policy).

The final sentence is excellent. An observation such as this will get the examiner on your side. It shows awareness and is pertinent to the question. Most significantly, it is not a line that has been rehearsed and repeated in the examination. This one sentence identifies the candidate as someone who is thinking about the question set during the exam itself and is drawing the threads together in order to make a sound judgement.

The price of the shares would be an issue. If share prices are low it might be possible to buy a firm cheaply (but harder to raise the money to do it).

⟦✏⟧ Too brief. This could have been an evaluative argument if set against some other factors (e.g. showing how the opportunity to acquire out-of-town sites would not have been worth it, on balance, if the share price was prohibitively high, thus losing the company too much money). Essays can sometimes test the skill with which a student uses ideas as much as the ability to come up with relevant ideas.

In conclusion, the factors to be considered will depend on the circumstances. If a profit can be made it is more likely to go ahead. Surveys indicate that the most successful take-overs are those involving firms of a similar size, and so this should be considered. It is much easier to understand the needs of a similar firm, and the two sets of employees are more likely to see it as a merger, rather than one company forcing its policies on another.

⟦✏⟧ The second sentence on profit is a bit weak without any other commentary but is still worth saying because it will nearly always be true.

There must be no detrimental effects. The firm will need a healthy cash flow, and there must be scope for efficiencies. In this case it may wish to rationalise the number of outlets, to cut costs without losing sales revenue. Alternatively, the take-over might work well if the two firms are not in direct competition (e.g. in different areas), but can benefit from economies of scale.

The final decision will depend on the owners of the two firms. The shareholders of the firm being taken over must be offered an attractive price for their shares, whilst the larger firm's shareholders must be convinced that it will benefit them too.

⟦✏⟧ The final paragraphs show good reasoning, but the arguments lack some application.

⟦✏⟧ This candidate shows a stronger grasp of theory than application, but there is a significant lack of detailed evaluation. All the same, there are a variety of valid arguments developed, with evidence of evaluation throughout and so this answer would be enough to secure a sound A grade.

■ ■ ■

Answer to question 3: candidate B

A firm will want to take over another firm in order to benefit from economies of scale.

⟦✏⟧ A very brief opener, but straight into a relevant concept.

There are many different types of economies of scale. Bulk-buying means that the firm can buy things cheaply. This means that it can cut its prices and force the competition out of the market. If the other firms become bankrupt it can put its price up and make even more money.

⟦✏⟧ Relevant analysis of a reason for a take-over earns the candidate some marks for analysis.

Without any competition it will be able to put more money back into the company for marketing and research and development. This will help it to make even more money.

⬛ The brevity of the paragraphs is making it difficult for the student to explain ideas fully. The candidate should reflect on such comments to discover whether there is more to say on the matter.

Taking over another firm will mean other economies of scale. The retailer will be able to advertise more. Using television and national newspapers will help it to reach more customers and become a household name. This will improve recognition of its name and encourage more people to buy its products. It will also have the money to spend on market research, finding out exactly what its customers want. This will mean that it can make goods specifically to suit the consumers, increasing its sales even more.

⬛ There is some further analysis of theory here, but the candidate is really finding lots of different ways to make the same point. If your essay plan (which you must set out before starting to write) only contains a list of the same or similar points, you should question whether you have interpreted the question correctly. The essay paper draws on the whole specification and is designed to allow you to display your understanding of the subject. It is therefore unlikely to have a very narrow focus, as that will restrict its accessibility. Questions are not set to catch students out, but to allow them to show their understanding, so make sure that you have made the right choice of essay before ploughing on.

New equipment can be bought. Investing in IT will help the retailer to improve the efficiency of its activities. Production, administration and stock control will all be improved, and so there will be less waste and inefficiency.

⬛ This is now becoming worrying. There has been no attempt to apply this answer to electrical retailers. The points made so far could apply to any type of company (and to firms that are just growing organically rather than through take-overs).

New methods such as kaizen and TQM can be introduced. These will lead to continuous improvement and better quality, which will, in turn, attract more customers. Higher prices can be charged if the products are of higher quality.

⬛ The essay has now moved further off the point and is following a common error. Whilst discussing one topic there is a tendency to move on to an associated topic, but one that does not necessarily relate to the question. Economies of scale are ways of improving efficiency; kaizen and TQM can also improve firms. However, whereas a take-over can lead to economies of scale there is no reason why a take-over should lead to kaizen or TQM. These methods can be used regardless of size.

Just-in-time methods will also improve stock control. Goods will be ordered just in time. This will eliminate the need for warehouses. This will save costs — there will be less rent to pay, fewer employees needed, and less chance of damage and theft. These savings will increase the profit of the firm. Under 'just-in-time' customers can give details of the exact product that they want. This will increase demand, allowing more profit to be made and ploughed back into research and development. Research and development will help the firm to discover consumer tastes and target new market segments.

☞ The question candidate B is answering has now changed to 'write anything you can on ways to improve efficiency'. The examiner would scrutinise this paragraph, in case there is something of relevance, but would be unable to find anything worthy of marks.

In conclusion, there are many factors that a firm should consider. The main factor is economies of scale. A large firm will be able to make more money by buying in bulk, and so lower its prices. It will also help it to borrow money more cheaply, use the best marketing media, carry out detailed market research and introduce IT. New methods such as lean production can be used. With all these changes the take-over will help the firm to improve its productivity and profit.

☞ There is an attempt to bring the answer back into focus, with a stab at a conclusion. In effect, much of this is a repeat, but some new points are noted that add to the earlier paragraphs. The final sentence is superficial and not supported.

Overall, this is a disappointing response, showing the need to plan an essay and to ensure that there is not too narrow an approach taken. There are marks given for application in all essays (20% of the total). In some instances this can be quite difficult if the question does not refer to a particular organisation. However, there is no reason for a failure to apply in this case. It appears that the question has not been read carefully, as no mention is made of electrical retailers in the answer. Invariably there are factors that could apply to all types of business, but reference to electrical retailers would at least have assured the examiner that an attempt to apply understanding was being made.

☞ **The arguments on economies of scale would receive some reward, and credit would be given for the conclusion. The marks earned on this question would not prevent a reasonable business report from securing an overall pass for the candidate, but in itself this response would be a U grade.**

Influences on marketing

Discuss the extent to which the actions of a firm's marketing department are affected by the objectives and activities of the other areas of the firm.

Answer to question 4: candidate A

In some Japanese firms there are no separate marketing departments. It is assumed that everyone is involved in marketing the business. This demonstrates that marketing must be integrated with other functions such as production, finance and personnel.

> An interesting opening, but it is not really proof. However, it does mean that the candidate is thinking in an integrated way.

No department can work separately from the other departments of the firm. The directors must decide on the corporate aims and objectives of the organisation. The directors responsible (e.g. the marketing director) will then translate these corporate objectives into departmental objectives. This hierarchy of objectives will make sure that all departments of the firm work towards the same targets. Objectives should provide a sense of direction, preventing a department following its own agenda.

> This is a top-rate section of the essay. It employs good understanding of business approaches in the context of the question, and helps the candidate to establish a logical structure.

Good objectives will be SMART: specific, measurable, achievable, realistic and timed. If the original objectives are too vague it may be possible for two departments to work in different directions, but only for a short period of time. If the marketing department is promoting its product as high quality, whilst the purchasing department is buying the cheapest materials possible, then it will soon become noticeable. Any disputes will be referred to the relevant managers who can then agree on a compromise.

> Good. The candidate has opened up the potential for inter-linking between departments and has avoided getting side-tracked into a discussion on objectives. The example really clarifies the candidate's thinking, illustrating the interdependence in a relevant manner.

In a new business there is likely to be more conflict than in an old business. An established business will have agreed on its main objectives and learned from experience how to deal with possible conflicts.

> There is real potential for evaluation here, but unfortunately the thinking has not been developed. This brevity considerably reduces the impact that could have been made.

question

For a firm to reach its objectives it is critical that each department cooperates with the others. A business is like a living organism, with all of the different parts playing their role in the welfare of the whole. The marketing department will need to discuss its strategies with the other departments. If a new image is required, it will need to be sure that purchasing can buy suitable raw materials. If it is targeting a new market it will need to check that distribution can deliver the products. A sudden increase in demand, achieved by a clever marketing campaign, could be a disaster if the other departments are not informed. There may not be enough workers employed or trained by personnel, or the production department could be unable to meet the demand or modify the product to match the one being marketed.

This is an excellent paragraph, really getting to the core of the essay. It opens with a very good analogy, but its main strength is the observation of the way in which the marketing department's actions are permeating across the company.

The same works in reverse. If the personnel department is unable to recruit workers, or if there is going to be a cutback in production, then the marketing department will need to change its plans, perhaps even cutting back on its promotions.

Although a briefer paragraph, it is adding quality to the answer by showing that the relationship works in other directions too. (There can be a temptation when answering a question on a certain topic or feature to elevate the importance of that topic or feature above all other factors. The candidate has resisted this temptation and has shown judgement in doing so.)

Other departments can help marketing, by suggesting new products or reporting back on feedback from customers.

Of course, the extent to which the different departments affect each other will depend on the culture of the firm. If power is heavily centralised, then each department will be given strict instructions on how to perform and what its targets will be. This will mean that the marketing department will be less influenced by the actions of the other departments; instead they will all be affected by the decisions and policies of the board or shareholders. In a more laissez-faire style of management or one in which each manager is empowered to make his or her own decisions, there is more of a probability that the marketing department's decisions will be affected by other departments. There will always be more risk of conflict between different departmental managers in this type of set-up, but the firm may think that, on balance, it is worthwhile. Empowered managers will be more motivated and be more aware of the factors affecting their strategies.

An excellent concluding paragraph, describing scenarios in which the inter-relationships between departments may vary. Overall, this answer would be awarded a solid A grade. The essay does, however, have a relatively narrow focus. In questions of this nature the finance department is a fruitful source of suggestions. Every business decision will have a financial repercussion, but it is possible to have issues that do not affect marketing or personnel, for example. However, this omission does not prevent this candidate from fully illustrating the potential for influence.

e **In a question that requires a candidate to show 'the extent to which' factor X is influenced by factor Y, there should be some consideration of the other factors that influence factor X. This response would have received a top grade A if it had drawn some comparison with factors such as customer response, the economy etc.**

■ ■ ■

Answer to question 4: candidate B

The marketing department's objectives and activities will be affected by external factors.

Market research is an essential element of marketing. This will not depend on the rest of the firm, but will be needed to find out the views and interests of the consumers. Market research will also inform the business of economic and social trends.

e This is a valid point, but a little worrying. At this early stage the candidate seems to have decided to rewrite the question and focus on other factors. There is a suspicion that this could be because the candidate feels more comfortable on external factors and is wanting to answer a question on them. Avoid this temptation. You must accept that the questions set may not be ideal for you.

Market research can be primary or secondary. Primary research is carried out by the business; secondary research uses information that has already been gathered for other purposes. Data can be quantitative (telling the business how much or how many items will be bought) or qualitative (telling them why people will buy, or what they are thinking).

e The candidate is showing knowledge, but the detail on market research is, at best, marginal to the question.

Market research will be the main influence on a company's marketing. Once it has gathered the information it will know how to promote its products and who is going to buy them. This will mean that it can target its customers by selecting the right media for advertising (e.g. using a comic for children or a football magazine for football fans). It can also design promotions or adverts to appeal to these customers.

e It is nice to see some recognition that market research is the responsibility of the marketing department, but the statement asks candidates to discuss different departments so this paragraph adds little to the answer.

The marketing department will also be influenced by the state of the economy. In a recession a company will lose sales, but in a boom its sales will be much higher. In a recession it could spend more on marketing to counter this loss of sales (although there may be less money available for advertising and marketing).

Social trends and consumer tastes will be a big influence on the marketing department. As more females have gone out to work, firms have reacted by producing more convenience goods. This is also connected to shopping habits, with longer hours and out-of-town centres that reflect the growth in car ownership. A marketing department must react to these changes. Ideally the firm should be pro-active, creating trends through its marketing so that it can be the first to meet a new demand.

Competition is an influence too. The marketing department will look closely at the actions of the competition. If the opposition brings out a new product then a business will want to release a me-too product to grab a share of the market. New advertising campaigns or methods of promotion will be copied too. This can be seen with supermarkets which have copied each other by introducing loyalty cards, new lines and home deliveries.

Government policy is another influence on marketing. Laws have been introduced to stop adverts lying about products (the Trade Descriptions Act) and there are rules that restrict advertising of cigarettes and alcohol.

> 🖉 Any one of these paragraphs would have been useful as an indication of how other factors influence the marketing department (and as such they would have enhanced the answer of candidate A, who failed to recognise these external factors). However, given that candidate B has not mentioned any other departments to date, these comments would be seen as a further drift away from the question.

It can be seen therefore that the main influence on a firm's marketing will be factors beyond its control. Firms exist within society and must be careful not to break laws or alienate customers. The skills of the marketing department will depend on the staff and how well they have been trained, and so the personnel department will have some influence, but in general the other departments will be employed to do their jobs separately. As long as the business is making a profit (and this depends on the marketing department more than the others), the marketing department should be free to do what it believes is best for the company without being told what to do by the other departments. Specialisation allows firms to become more efficient.

> 🖉 The reference to the personnel department is helpful but is too little too late. There has been some attempt to evaluate, but it is weak because of the absence of any other points with which to contrast the ideas. The absence of supporting evidence for the view that the marketing department is the major wealth creator means that this point cannot be credited. There appears to be no logic to the inclusion of the final line.

✌ This answer would be a **U grade**. The candidate has ignored the wording of the question. Whilst each of the points made could be considered to be a relevant observation, overall the answer lacks relevance because none of the factors mentioned are directly linked to the title.

If the question had read 'Discuss the extent to which the actions of a firm's marketing department are affected by external factors?', this would have been a good answer. However, this was not the question. A general 'discuss the factors ...' style of question does give some leeway, but a question that refers directly to a specific influence (in this case the other areas of the firm) must be answered with reference to those areas. If the candidate sincerely believes that the other areas are not important, then evidence must be provided to support that view. Simply ignoring a part of the question is not the right approach.

Information technology

> To what extent is an understanding of information technology critical to a firm's success?

Answer to question 5: candidate A

There are many factors that could contribute to the success of a firm. In this essay I shall be examining the importance of IT.

Firstly, we need to define success. Firms do not all have the same aims and so it is not possible to state with certainty a definition of success. A working definition is that success or achievement could be measured by the extent to which a firm achieves its aims and objectives.

✍ The opening paragraph does not say much, but this is an excellent second paragraph. The decision to define success is shrewd, as this is an important element of any conclusion for this essay. There is evidence of evaluation already.

Major objectives will include a profit target (unless the firm is a charity), the provision of a good service or product, growth, reputation, or meeting the needs of workers or society.

Whatever aim or objective is chosen, it is clear that efficiency will be a key measure of success. An efficient organisation will have the resources to raise the finance necessary to guarantee that it reaches its other objectives.

✍ These two paragraphs provide further clarification for the reader. This is a skilful opening as it legitimately widens the scope of the essay, allowing a range of arguments to be presented. However, one should be careful not to change the question. There is always a temptation to twist a question in order to include favourite topics. This can lead to irrelevance.

How can IT help a firm to become more efficient? Information technology has been a central part of the communication revolution. Society places a much higher value on information and expects to be kept well informed. IT provides firms with the capability to communicate rapidly. Even though web sales have not fully taken off, the number of 'hits' on company websites shows the frequency with which people make contact. Information, such as price lists, product availability and opening times, can be immediately accessed by potential customers. This gives a firm a competitive advantage over rivals which do not provide such a service.

✍ This is rather descriptive early on but the answer eventually gets to the point, and the final sentence ensures that the comments are interpreted in the context of the question.

It should be noted that there are many people not connected to the web, but its use is very high in Britain compared to most countries, and it is heavily used by the market segments with high incomes or earnings potential. In this respect I would say that IT is critical to a firm's future success, even if it is less relevant at the moment.

✎ Here is excellent evaluation again (although there has not actually been much analysis so far in the answer). While evaluation is more noticeable in a conclusion, the opportunities to bring it into the answer through particular observations should not be underestimated.

The use of IT in production is very important. The speed and accuracy of production can be improved dramatically by computers. For manufacturing there has been a move away from labour-intensive methods to capital-intensive production, because computerisation allows a standardised, high-quality product to be produced very cheaply. This change has been more pronounced in high-wage economies such as the USA and Germany. In the Third World, labour costs are much lower (and IT equipment more difficult to obtain). It could therefore be argued that the importance of IT does depend on the state of the economy and the wealth of the country. Investment in IT should enable a firm to improve its competitiveness.

✎ Very good application is displayed by relating IT to different countries, and analysis is evident through the reasoning applied. The final conclusion in the penultimate sentence shows sound judgement. This candidate is demonstrating a keen awareness of the importance of IT.

IT has also led to changes in production methods. Gone are the days of the Model T Ford (any colour you like as long as it's black). With IT even mass production can be adjusted to make variations in the product, increasing its appeal to the market.

✎ This is a nice idea (and a good example), but it is not exploited to the full. It could have led to further consideration of the growing importance of IT to specific firms.

Up to this point the arguments have been one-sided. This is excusable because few people would contest the idea that IT has brought benefits to firms, and so evaluation can focus on the relative importance of it to differing types of business, rather than contriving to provide a balanced view when such a balance is unrealistic.

IT can be seen to be an important factor in a firm's success, but it can also contribute to failure. Its introduction must be planned carefully, so that the maximum benefit is gained. If it is introduced without planning it may not prove to be useful. There should be a needs analysis first, identifying exactly how the firm can benefit from IT. This will make sure that the right systems and equipment are purchased. It is generally accepted that firms and individuals have a tendency to buy IT equipment that is capable of doing far more than they need, thus wasting a lot of money. However, buying a system that is too simple is going to cause more expensive problems. There also needs to be training of staff — it is no use having the latest equipment if nobody knows how to use it.

> Excellent. On top of the earlier evaluation, the candidate has now presented a well-argued point that does provide some balance of opinion. There is also an assessment of factors that can help (or hinder) the success of IT usage.

IT dates quickly and so an organisation should be aware of the costs. An investment appraisal should be carried out to see if it is worthwhile. There is no point in buying a computer if it is only used for 1 year and its payback is 18 months.

Is IT critical to a firm's success? It can be seen that it is very important, but then so are a number of other aspects of running a business. A case could be argued that financial planning is more important, or possibly the training of the workforce. (After all, workers need to understand how to use their computers.)

> Having argued the case for IT as a source of success and then shown some of its limitations, the candidate is now concluding by painting a broader picture. The extent to which IT is a factor that is critical to success does relate, ultimately, to the significance of other influences. Therefore, it is good practice to compare its influence to the influence of other factors (but not to the extent that the essay loses sight of the influence of IT). This paragraph is well-reasoned and finally relates back to information technology.

The importance of IT will depend on the firm. Some personal services (such as plumbers) could survive without a computer, but it would be impossible for a bank to function without a sophisticated IT system. What is certain is that IT is becoming more critical to the success of most businesses and, as the use of home computers, WAP phones and internet access increases, its importance will continue to grow. It may not be critical to the plumber, but its presence will help him to succeed.

> The final paragraph wraps the essay up nicely, making further observations whilst showing how its impact can vary. There can be a tendency for students to over-generalise ('everyone gets hit badly in a recession'; 'all Japanese firms use the same production methods'). The conclusion here shows how the impact will vary and, whilst this may not be profound, it is an observation worth making.

> **This essay is particularly strong on evaluation, despite the relatively brief conclusion. It has also focused sufficiently on the basics, indicating the benefit of moving quickly up the levels rather than identifying dozens of different bullet points. This is a good A-grade script.**

E6

ssay question

Ratio analysis

How useful is ratio analysis to a business?

Answer to question 6: candidate A

Ratio analysis allows a business to evaluate its financial performance. Whatever the aims and objectives of an organisation, it must be able to manage its finances. Shareholders and owners of private sector firms will want to see some profit in return for the finance that they have provided. Even charities must control their finances in order to meet their main aim — to maximise the amounts of money that they give to good causes.

> Although the opening paragraph is rather disjointed, it sets the scene well, justifying the use of ratios to many types of organisation. This may have been more effective after a definition and demonstration of the use of ratios, but it still serves its purpose.

I shall answer this question by studying the benefits provided by ratio analysis. These will be set against the difficulties and limitations of using ratios in order to reach a conclusion.

> This is a good plan, showing a logical approach (as long as it is actually carried out). However, it is not really needed in the essay as such. It may reassure the examiner, but only if the approach is actually used.

Ratios can be used to measure profitability, liquidity, gearing and financial efficiency. There are also ratios that help shareholders to measure the success of their investment.

> Good. This is a helpful introduction and shows that the writer recognises the varied nature of ratio analysis.

The main profitability ratio is the return on capital employed (ROCE%). This is calculated as follows:

$$\frac{\text{net profit} \times 100}{\text{capital employed}} = \text{ROCE }\%$$

> Defining the formula helps to clarify the candidate's understanding and this will be rewarded, but the key factor is to demonstrate a recognition of what the ratios are depicting.

The higher the percentage the better. Businesses will compare themselves to competitors. They can also see if their ROCE % is higher than it was in the previous year. The capital employed equals the funds used by the business. If it had put this money into a bank it could have received, say, 6% interest without any risk, and so this would be a minimum target. In the UK the average is over 13%, but in some industries you would expect more. This is one of the limitations of ratio analysis — it is not always possible to be certain what a ratio is showing.

The opening sentences show excellent analysis and this is continued through most of the paragraph. There is then a relevant identification of a limitation, but this is not really explained. Consequently, the section ends in an anti-climax, with the examiner wanting to award marks but being unable to find the explanation to merit this. Believe it or not, examiners do like giving marks!

There are other ratios that measure profitability — the net profit to sales % and the gross profit to sales %. As profitability is a major objective of any firm, the analysis of these ratios is essential in measuring the success of the firm.

This is relevant to the question, but in the particular circumstances of an examination room it is not the ideal approach. The candidate has shown an awareness of profitability ratios in the previous paragraph. Given the limitations of time, it would be more productive to add a different dimension by moving on to a different type of ratio (such as liquidity) or looking for some limitations.

Liquidity shows the ability of a firm to pay its short-term liabilities. It is estimated that 20% of firms that cease to trade do so because of poor liquidity rather than a lack of profitability. This can happen because firms build up high stock levels, or buy fixed assets because they are doing well, but then find themselves short of cash and so they cannot pay the bills. Liquidity can be measured by the current ratio: current assets/current liabilities.

Odd snippets of information (such as the second sentence) can improve an answer. This part of the essay shows a good understanding of liquidity, confirming in the examiner's mind that the candidate is aware of the concepts involved, and is applying and analysing effectively.

The last sentence defines the current ratio. Is this valid? (The current ratio is not on the A-level business studies specification, which uses the acid test ratio as a way to demonstrate liquidity.) The answer is 'yes', if it is relevant. A-level specifications cannot include every possible business concept, so certain terms and concepts are not mentioned. The absence of a concept means that you will not specifically be asked to calculate a ratio such as the current ratio, but it does not prevent you from introducing it if it contributes towards the quality of an answer. The specification is not intended to constrain a student, and so the use of this ratio will be credited (and welcomed, in fact).

If the business has twice as many current assets as liabilities then this ratio is 2:1. This would be ideal, showing that the business could easily pay all its debts. In fact, anything above 1.5:1 would be seen as fine.

The concept has been applied appropriately.

Gearing measures the degree to which a firm's capital is borrowed rather than provided by shareholders. Interest must be paid on borrowed money, but it is possible to pay a zero dividend to shareholders in a bad year. The higher the percentage of capital that is borrowed, the bigger the risk for the business — in a bad year it may be unable to pay and face liquidation.

> Another clear indication that the candidate understands and can apply ratio analysis. Up to this point the content, application and analysis have been very good. However, there has been little evidence of critical consideration. The candidate should now be focusing on a closer examination of the relative usefulness of ratios.

Financial efficiency ratios are less important. They examine particular aspects of the finances and so will tell a firm if its rate of stock turnover is good or bad, or whether its debtors are taking too long to pay up.

> These are valid ideas, but they are not really adding value to the answer for the reasons identified earlier.

There are limitations though. Ratios are historical — they look at the past and that is not always a good predictor of the future. Accounts can also be window dressed to improve performance, although there are rules that limit this and an improvement this year may mean that next year looks less impressive. Profit quality is another issue. If the profit is made from selling fixed assets, it can disguise a poor performance (using operating profit rather than net profit will overcome this problem).

> Good. The move on to limitations is helping to produce the balance required. There is judgement shown in these arguments too, through recognition that window dressing has its constraints and in the final sentence.

The major drawback of ratios is that they assume that firms have only one objective — to maximise profit. Any conclusions drawn must therefore be treated with caution. If a business is targeting growth, then maximising revenue might be a more important aim and so decisions may be taken that might be causing liquidity problems in the short term.

> A good analysis of the limitations.

Detailed analysis of other activities is also needed — expenditure on research and development or marketing campaigns may be useful for the future but actually worsen financial performance in the short term.

> Recognition of the need to consider other elements is well illustrated in this paragraph.

For these reasons ratio analysis must not be carried out in isolation. Used on its own it can be helpful, but it may lead to inappropriate conclusions. If its results are compared carefully, and a study of the other aspects of running a business are also included, it can be a very useful tool. It is better to have the information so that possible problems can be deduced, but an efficient firm will have introduced methods that should prevent bad ratios happening in the first place.

At last there is a concentration on evaluation, but it has been dealt with rather too briefly. There are some nice observations here, but justice has not been done to them as the candidate does not appear to have left sufficient time.

The candidate has got carried away with displaying knowledge and reveals a weakness in time management. It is very tempting to continue with a line of thought when there is more that can be said, but 40 minutes is not enough time to say everything. A skill being tested is the ability to select the most important items. With 40% of the marks for an essay being awarded for evaluation (knowledge, application and analysis are awarded 20% each), it is essential that sufficient time is devoted to evaluation, even if this means omitting a particular fact or piece of analysis.

Having said that, the essay shows excellence in all of the non-evaluative skills, and scores reasonably in that skill too. Consequently, this response would be worth a good A-grade.